"Anxiety is part of the 'broken brain' syndrome that millions of Americans suffer from. Conventional medicine can mask the symptoms, but it doesn't tackle the root cause. That's what the total mind-body system of qigong does. In this groundbreaking workbook, Master Kam Chuen Lam shows us how to use our own life-force energy to lift our minds and bodies to a new level of wellness. Open this book to any page and you'll find it's one of the most practical, helpful, and friendly guidebooks to your own well-being you can imagine."

—**Mark Hyman, MD**, author of the #1 *New York Times* bestseller,
The Blood Sugar Solution

"Master Kam Chuen Lam's workbook is a valuable resource for anyone dealing with anxiety, worry, or stress. The ancient healing exercises he shares from decades of experience are presented in a format that is easy to understand, learn, and practice. Having worked with some of these exercises I can personally say they cultivate more peace, calm, and body awareness. This is a book I will be recommending to many of my clients for years to come!"

—**Tahir Bhatti, MD**, wellness physician, director of Integrative Holistic Services, and associate clinical professor in the department of psychology at the University of California, San Diego

"In a world where everyone experiences stress and worry, what a gift it is to read *The Qigong Workbook for Anxiety*. Master Kam Chuen Lam introduces readers to the ancient tradition of qigong in a friendly and accessible way. He teaches simple yet potent methods for relaxing both physical and emotional tension. His instructions are revolutionary in that he encourages us not to reject feelings of anxiety. Instead, by practicing these qigong exercises we become aware of our greater energy field and learn how to regulate our nervous system even when tension arises. This book is for anyone who wants to tap into their inner strength and live a calmer, healthier life."

—**Amy Conway, MPH**, senior managerial consultant for Kaiser Permanente in Northern California

"Having worked for over thirty years in a busy and demanding dental practice, I am no stranger to stress at work. I can, without hesitation, attribute my current well-being largely to my daily practice and enjoyment of qigong. Being calm as a practitioner, I am able to bring harmony to the way I run my practice and patients enjoy the peaceful atmosphere. I strongly believe that Master Kam Chuen Lam's unique lineage, wisdom, and extensive knowledge [make this book] a must-have for all busy and stressed professionals who also want to remain truly healthy whilst having to endure daily challenges at work and home."

—**Thye Yeoh**, qigong student and dental practitioner in the UK

"Do not let the simplicity of the exercises in this book fool you. ... I work as the compliance director of a major financial firm in London—a highly stressful job—and I can vouch from my own experience for the profundity of these exercises and the enormous wisdom of Master Kam Chuen Lam's teaching."

—**Charles Beck**, qigong student and director of compliance, Lond

"True health is more than exercise and good nutrition. It includes peace of mind. Those who possess it glow and seem to have access to a wellspring of pure energy. If you've ever wondered how to become such a person, qigong Master Kam Chuen Lam can guide you there."

—**Susan Piver**, founder of the Open Heart Project

"Qigong combines two approaches to treating anxiety that are known to work: exercise and mindfulness. This highly accessible and readable workbook should help many more people enjoy the benefits of qigong."

—**Elizabeth Murray**, general practitioner and professor of emergency health and primary care at the University of London, UK

"This book comes at the right time. More than ever, employees and managers are struggling to keep up with the ever-increasing speed and constantly rising demands of business life. The ensuing stress and burnout is literally killing people. Western approaches to dealing with the resulting issues have reached their limits. Master Kam Chuen Lam's workbook is addressing the root cause—anxiety—in a new way. It is based on age-old Chinese wisdom and Lam's own life's work devoted to the study of human energy. I highly recommend it to everyone who wants to be successful in the long run."

—**Thomas Apfel**, corporate account manager at IBM

"Master Kam Chuen Lam's new book about dealing with anxiety is a revelation on its own. During my daily interaction with dental patients, I come across a big percentage of anxiety cases. I have been aiming to incorporate Master Kam Chuen Lam's relaxation techniques during treatment. As a result, patients often relax so much that they're telling us when they get off the dental chair that they feel as if they had a good rest! It is without a doubt, that in this book, various daily issues are addressed in an effective manner. Conventional Western medicine has no ammunition to combat stress or anxiety for everyday life or work. Look no further, Master Kam Chuen Lam's new book provides you with the essential elements to survive today's hectic lifestyle and emerge unscathed with simple techniques. It's the first time I've come across such an informative and to-the-point read. … It is a beacon of hope in today's jungle."

—**Maria Maliderou, DDS, MSc**, qigong student and dentist based in London, UK

"Stand, be still, and master anxiety. Master Kam Chuen Lam's highly-engaging *The Qigong Workbook for Anxiety* is a gift for anyone struggling with fear."

—**Gary Lopes Cunha, LMFT, LPCC**, outpatient psychiatry clinician for Kaiser Permanente in Northern California

"Master Kam Chuen Lam's qigong exercises are like a warm internal shower that relaxes, yet energizes. They seem a perfect antidote to the anxieties of life and aging. Getting older myself and working with elders, as I do, I can attest to their powerful benefits. This workbook is a wonderful guide and support for new and experienced practitioners alike."

—**Vicki Giella**, qigong participant and former manager of the Senior HelpLine, a telephone assistance service for elders, their families, and caregivers

The Qigong Workbook *for* Anxiety

Powerful Energy Practices to
Rebalance Your Nervous System
and Free Yourself from Fear

Master Kam Chuen Lam

New Harbinger Publications, Inc.

Publisher's Note

This publication is designed to provide accurate and authoritative information in regard to the subject matter covered. It is sold with the understanding that the publisher is not engaged in rendering psychological, financial, legal, or other professional services. If expert assistance or counseling is needed, the services of a competent professional should be sought.

Distributed in Canada by Raincoast Books

Copyright © 2014 by Kam Chuen Lam
              New Harbinger Publications, Inc.
              5674 Shattuck Avenue
              Oakland, CA 94609
              www.newharbinger.com

Cover design by Sara Christian
Acquired by Jess O'Brien
Edited by Jennifer Eastman

Library of Congress Cataloging-in-Publication Data on file

Printed in the United States of America

16   15   14

10   9   8   7   6   5   4   3   2   1   First printing

Contents

Dedication

With profound gratitude for the countless masters
who discovered the secrets of human energy
and shared their knowledge of this art,
for my beloved late master, Yu Yongnian,
and for my very dear wife and sons,
I dedicate this book and its healing power
to human well being and a world at peace.

Foreword

By Professor Yu Yongnian

Honorary member of the Council of the Association of Qigong Science of the People's Republic of China, former adviser to the American-Chinese Qigong Association, and honorary chairperson of the Da Cheng Chuan Zhan Zhuang Chi Kung Research Groups (Europe).

Anxiety is a problem everywhere in the world today. In the course of my lifetime, I have seen the world speed up. Everything is affected. Speed has changed the nature of people's work, travel, communications, and almost every field of life. Even their family lives have changed. This acceleration has also affected the human psyche. Our nervous systems feel the constant impact of the instability and violence of life around us. Millions of people are suffering from tremendous tension. It affects their health as individuals, and it has a serious effect on our societies as well.

The intensity of what we are experiencing is new, but anxiety itself is not.

The earliest texts of the natural scientists of my country, dating back thousands of years, examined this problem and talked about calming the mind. Perhaps the most famous is the *Tao Te Ching* of the great master Laozi, who wrote:

Rest your mind ...
Do not tinkle like slivers of jade
Or bang around like stone shards ...
From stillness and tranquility comes the order of the universe.

Laozi's writings include some of the earliest known references to qigong, the art of cultivating the internal energy of the human being. I have studied this art for over seventy years. I had the privilege of being a student, in my early twenties, of the Grand Master Wang Xiang Zhai. He brought this art out of the realms of secrecy into the light of public teaching. He taught the rare qigong system known as *zhan zhuang*. It is the most powerful of all the systems for cultivating human energy. But it involves no external movement at all. This makes it unique.

Practicing zhan zhuang qigong changed my life. At the time, I was a young dentist who suffered from a great deal of tension. I experienced it in my upper back as I treated my patients. All that changed after I started learning this art. Under my master's guidance, I went deeper. I began to see the inner significance and power of this art. I saw the transformation that its healing and calming power could have on people's lives.

During the many decades I have practiced zhan zhuang qigong, I have also seen it change the lives of countless people who have been my students. Some people may think that, since this is part of China's cultural heritage, it is only helpful to Chinese people. Not at all. I have had the good fortune to teach in other countries in Asia, as well as in America and Europe. My experience has shown me that zhan zhuang qigong is a precious treasure in the heritage of all humanity.

I am therefore delighted that Kam Chuen Lam, my disciple, has written this book to show people how they can use this ancient art to help them with their anxiety. Together, we bridge East and West. I studied Western medicine in my youth, becoming a professor of dentistry. Kam Chuen Lam studied traditional Chinese herbalism and bonesetting. We have used our different backgrounds to create a pathway for people everywhere to study qigong, which we have in common.

He first came to study with me in Beijing. After that, I went to London to supervise the production of his first book, *The Way of Energy*. It introduced the zhan zhuang system of qigong to the West. One of my favorite photos was taken on that trip. It shows me standing with one of the royal guards in the city.

This year, a large delegation of Kam Chuen Lam's students from nearly twenty countries around the world came to Beijing to show me their progress. I was delighted to be part of a huge energy circle with them. As I felt the current of their energy, which I was part of myself, I felt our circle was a powerful symbol. It made me appreciate not only the progress of those students, but also the progress of our whole system of zhan zhuang qigong. It has come a long way since I helped introduce it into hospitals in China in the 1950s. At that time, we saw how helpful it was in the treatment of chronic diseases. Now we know that it is helpful for people in all conditions of health.

The Qigong Workbook for Anxiety will open up a new chapter. It shows, step by step, how this ancient art can be used in our own age for one of the most common disorders that people are now suffering from—the pain of the heart and mind caused by anxiety.

—Professor Yu Yongnian

Beijing, 2013

Age 94

Master Lam

Acknowledgments

This workbook has a long history, and many people have made it possible. I would like to express particular gratitude to my grand master, Wang Xiang Zhai, who courageously decided that the treasures of this tradition, which were passed on as a secret transmission over the centuries, should be made public.

My own master, Professor Yu Yongnian, graciously accepted me as a student—even though he was taking a personal risk in doing so in the dangerous days of the Cultural Revolution in China, when ancient arts were under threat. He was a constant and powerful force in my life; and to the extent that I have been able to experience the depths of this art, it is thanks to his deep practice, immense skill, and great kindness. He wrote the foreword to this book just before his death in October 2013. As my senior students wrote in a funeral tribute to him, "We have lost not only our grand master, but a noble human being."

My wife, Kaisin, has stood by me through all the years in which I have studied this art and endeavored to bring it to the world beyond China. Without her, what I have done would not have been possible. I would also like to thank my sons, Tin Yuan, Tin Yu, and Tin Hun, for their support, understanding, and unending help.

Lastly, I would like to thank all my students who have made a sincere effort to learn this art and who have remained with me over these years. In particular, I would like to thank my devoted student Richard Reoch, who has helped me with the planning and writing of many of my books, and who has been my constant companion in my efforts to bridge East and West.

Auspiciously, we were introduced to New Harbinger Publications and their acquisitions editor, Jess O'Brien, who had, unknown to us, been reading and studying my books for over a decade. I am deeply grateful for New Harbinger's willingness to help me bring this healing wisdom into the world in this form.

Qi

This is the Chinese character for "qi," pronounced "chee." It represents the invisible, all-pervasive, and palpable life force of the universe. The top of the ideogram represents a cooking pot. Underneath it are four strokes that symbolize fire. The pot is filled with boiling water and steam is rising from it.

Just as steam is capable of powering engines and other devices, so the power of qi enables us to do anything we want. It is like pressure—air pressure, water pressure, wind pressure. In the human being, it takes the form of personal power, present throughout our being and visible in the photographs that scientists are now capable of taking of our aura.

The power of qi is capable of breaking through the blockages in our energetic pathways, such as those that we experience as the paralysis of anxiety or the congealed stagnation of fear.

Introduction

This workbook offers anyone who suffers from anxiety a step-by-step way to transform that agitated energy into resilient inner strength. You are introduced to the ancient art of harmonizing your own internal energy and drawing strength from the energy around you. This art is known as "qigong" (pronounced "chee gung"), which means "internal energy work." Qigong is part of the world's oldest continuous system of natural medicine, developed in China over centuries.

Part 1: Energy, Anxiety, and Inner Strength

Part 1 introduces you to a different way of thinking about yourself. In qigong, you are seen as a complete field of energy—similar to the current thinking of atomic physics. The energy of your whole being is what is studied and strengthened.

Qigong is based on the truth that each person is unique and to be respected. Your feelings, attitudes, and behaviors—including their deepest psychological patterns—are part of your total energy field. Fearful and difficult feelings are not regarded as enemies but as part of the whole. Working with your complete field of energy, rather than splitting it up, is at the heart of this system of well-being.

Part 2: Your Personal Energy Field

You are first introduced to your energy field and are given simple exercises that help you get a feel for it. Anxiety, worries, and difficulties of all sorts make us tense, and when we are tense, our ability to feel what is happening in our bodies is blocked. This makes it very difficult to actually feel how tense we are. But after a little tension release, our natural sensitivity begins to be restored. Those natural feelings are what we need to remember and reacquaint ourselves with. It will help you learn how to use your bodily experience to develop a mental "imprint" of tension release. You can use the charts in this section of the workbook to help you track your personal experience.

Part 3: Developing Your Inner Strength

Once you start to feel that you are working with your energy in a different way, not resisting moments of anxiety and other strong emotions but embracing them within the larger flow of your body's energy field, you learn how to strengthen and cultivate the natural energy you possess. This increases your stamina, resilience, and inner strength. What previously made you panic is now experienced as an energy blip passing through the far larger, vibrant field of your total being. The gentle exercises and postures described in this part of the book are surprisingly simple and can be done without any equipment at all. Charts in this part of the book help you keep track of your daily energy training and the way you are using your new awareness of energy to work with your emotions from the perspective of inner strength.

Part 4: Using the Power of Your Senses

Often, when we are suddenly gripped by anxiety, we have no time to reflect, meditate, or do calm breathing. How can we use the immediate energy of the world around us to be more grounded and less swept away? In part 4, you are introduced to the centuries-old tradition of using the power of sight, sound, smell, touch, and taste to influence your experience in subtle and profound ways. Our sensory experience is also part of the play and flow of our energy—and a gateway to connecting with the constant movement of energy around us.

In this section, with the help of step-by-step instructions and charts, you learn simple methods that help balance and harmonize your mental, emotional, and physical experience. The methods form a path that strengthens and increases the flexibility of your whole nervous system. You are encouraged to do this in very personal ways—to become the world's leading expert on your own experience.

Part 5: Working with the Energy Around You

Anxiety can have the effect of closing us down. We can feel claustrophobic and alone with our agitation. No matter how we feel, we do not exist in isolation. Each of us exists in a vast, constantly dynamic field of energy: the world around us. We experience many different environments every day—home, office, and the natural world—all with their own energies, all influencing us in different ways. In this final part of the workbook, you learn ways of understanding and using these energies—and also what you can do to protect yourself from harmful energies, which are common in this age of high-energy technology. You will also learn simple methods for developing and sharing positive energy with others, as well as how families and friends can help generate vibrant and healthy energy fields.

The Lineage

The art of qigong is the result of human inquiry, experimentation, and practice stretching over centuries. What I am sharing with you has been handed down in secret—literally from person to person—as masters passed on their wisdom to their students. It is only in modern times that it has become public. In passing on an art like this, it has always been important to know that the transmission is authentic. For this reason, I would like you to know the story of my lineage, and I hope you will find time to read these pages. Knowing this will be important to you—especially if someone asks you about qigong, where it came from, and why you are practicing it.

Before You Begin

You will be working with your own energy field—that makes it very personal. It will help if you pay close attention to your experience as you try the various exercises and suggestions. To help you do this, charts located throughout the workbook prompt you to think about and record what you are doing and how you are feeling. This way, you can be your own natural scientist, examining your own experience and deciding what is working best for you.

Many people, when they start qigong, worry about whether they are doing the right thing, whether they are making progress, or (worst of all) whether they might be making a serious mistake. Guess what—that makes them anxious. Don't beat yourself up. All the exercises and suggestions in this book have been developed and tested over centuries, and I have only included things that, in my experience, have proved helpful to my own students—who come from all over the world, all backgrounds, and all ages.

It's natural to wonder if you are making "progress," but actually, this idea is not really part of the qigong tradition. What happens when you practice qigong is very natural and almost imperceptible, the way a plant grows, day by day. If you feel impatient, uncertain, or frustrated, because you can't see or feel any progress, please note that down as part of your experience. Your natural energy will help you ride it all the better if you are fully aware of what's happening on your journey.

Some people like to read books from the back to the front. So you might be reading this introduction last! That's all right. I have tried to sprinkle this kind of advice throughout the workbook. You do not have to do the exercises and suggestions in this book in a strict order. I suggest you look first at part 1 and follow the exercises and suggestions there first. But if you have already tried some of the practices for your senses from part 4 or some exercises from another part of the book, please continue to do that, working with whatever has the best effect on you. You can add the exercises and suggestions from the earlier parts of the book—they will contribute to the power of whatever else you are doing.

If you want to develop a qigong routine, you can find one outlined in part 3. Following it is entirely up to you. You can also simply experiment with whatever you wish from this book and try to incorporate it into your lifestyle. If you do decide to follow a qigong routine, normally I recommend doing it in the morning. If you do it before breakfast, it is a good idea to drink a little warm water (not tea or coffee) before you start. If you have breakfast first, you should allow a short gap before you start your training. If you do your training at night, it is best to do it in a room with a light on. Preferably, there should be some source of fresh air in the room. If it is not possible to open a window, at least try not to practice in a room where the air is stale.

Different people have different sensations when they start to practice qigong. It's common to feel warm, even hot. You might find yourself shaking a little—sometimes a lot—as your energy wakes up. Sometimes it's hard to sit or stand still, especially if you are always on the go. Those sensations are part of the practice. Whatever you experience is the result of the deep power of qigong.

Your Personal Responsibility

It is important that you understand that the advice I am offering in this book is a contribution toward your personal training and development. I have done everything in my ability to ensure that this book will be beneficial to your health and well-being. But I cannot possibly know every reader individually, and therefore I cannot adapt the instructions for each person.

It is therefore important that you understand that, owing to causes completely beyond my control, you might experience difficulties that you might feel are somehow connected with your qigong practice. People have been using my books for over twenty years, and no one has ever reported experiencing this. Nevertheless, please take personal responsibility and check that there is no medical reason to prevent you from undertaking the practices in this book.

What to Do if You Have a Problem Using Qigong

If at any time in your qigong practice you feel heat or pressure rushing to your head, start to have a headache, or feel dizzy or faint, you should immediately do the practice "Gathering Your Energy" (located in part 1) three times, slowly and carefully. You can do it three more times if you want to. Finish with a qi massage to the face and neck (located in part 5). Then completely relax and rest, breathing naturally.

A Further Word of Welcome

Now that we have gone over all these useful tips in preparation for using this book, I would like to welcome you as you begin to explore this ancient art. The contemplation and inner work are personal and unique to each person. It is your own journey, working with the energy within you and around you. This art has been handed down from master to student in an unbroken succession of person-to-person transmission for over two thousand years. Through the pages of this book, I am delighted to extend this human wisdom now to you.

A Quick Check Before You Start

We'll be working with anxiety using the mind-body connection. The physical effects of anxiety in your body affect your mind—your thoughts and emotions—just as your thoughts and emotions have a direct effect on your body. We will be reading the physical signs throughout this workbook, so it will be useful to catalogue them now. But please don't mistake this for a physical check-up. In the centuries-old tradition of qigong, mind and body are inseparable, and we use each one to help the other. Please take a minute or two to record how you are feeling in this chart. You will want to come back to this chart later and see what you wrote.

Breathing	How does your breathing feel?		
	Fast or slow?	Shallow or deep?	Easy or difficult?

Head and Neck	How does the area of your head and neck feel?		
	Tense or relaxed?	Stiff or loose?	Are you having any pain?

Eyes	How do your eyes feel?		
	Relaxed or pressured?	Lively or dull?	Is there any soreness?

Mouth	How does your mouth feel?		
	Calm or tense?	Too wet or dry?	Do you clench or grind your teeth?

Shoulders and chest	How do your shoulders and chest feel?		
	Open or constricted?	Upright or hunched?	Are you having any pain or congestion?

Abdomen	How does your abdomen feel?		
	Tight or relaxed?	Trouble eating or digesting?	Bowel difficulties?

Lower back	How does your lower back feel?		
	Strong or weak?	Too tight or loose?	Any pain?

Temperature	Are you feeling any uncomfortable sensations during the day or night—too hot or too cold? Is any particular part of your body experiencing this?

Your emotions	Are you experiencing any strong emotional state at this point? Is there a particular emotional pattern that you regularly experience?		
	Anxiety or fear?	Emotional numbness?	Other feelings?

The Bridge

The character for "bridge" literally means "arch" and is pronounced "kiew." Its complexity expresses the dynamic and multifaceted quality of a bridge—the quality of all that is involved in crossing a gap.

All bridges are complex. They require a combination of materials to take the strain of those who cross them. They also need flexibility. Whether made of bamboo, wood, metal, or stone, bridges need to be able to yield. A bridge allows communication—allowing people and ideas to move from one place to another. A bridge is also always open, offering itself; anyone can pass over a bridge.

A conversation can be a bridge. A person can be a bridge. An ambassador is a bridge. This book is a bridge.

PART 1

Energy, Anxiety, and Inner Strength

"Engaging, Not Avoiding"

One of my students in California is a counselor for a major health organization that treats millions of people throughout the United States. In addition to being a health professional in the Western tradition, he has been studying internal energy work with me. We often talk about the tremendous health problems that people of all walks of life are faced with day after day in our modern world.

He has encouraged me to offer what I can from my years of studying, practicing, and teaching qigong, because he believes this kind of total energy work is part of what is desperately needed in these difficult times. "Your tradition is a lineage of healer-warriors," he said. "You teach the mastery of anxiety through the Way of Energy. It is possible to live a vibrant and meaningful life even with anxiety and in the midst of all the challenges we face."

He told me that the ancient tradition of qigong was very much in line with what many health-care professionals are now thinking. "We need a perspective that emphasizes mindfulness, not avoidance," he told me. "Avoidance in our day and age is packaged as feeling better, avoiding internal experience. This approach is reinforced with pharmacy ads promising happiness. The anxious usually need energy, but more importantly, they need a willingness to engage their worst fears if they are to have a chance of mastering them. Many have limited lives, because they want to 'feel better'—by not experiencing anxiety. Paradoxically, this attitude keeps them chronically anxious in the long term."

In the ancient tradition of qigong, which is a way of working with all forms of energy, trying to avoid our actual experience is not considered healthy. Whatever we are experiencing is part of the total energetic field, both around us and in us. The more we are open to it, the more power we can draw from it.

Thus this book offers what may seem a different approach to working with anxiety. It works with the full energy spectrum of the human being, including all our experience, as well as the vast energy field that surrounds us at all times.

The Energy of Anxiety—Bridging Two Cultures

Anxiety is an age-old phenomenon. All human beings experience it. It takes place in all cultures. All medical and health-care systems offer ways of helping us deal with it. At the same time, it is hard to define. It is an elusive vibration that takes many forms.

It is evoked in one of the oldest classics of world culture, the *Tao Te Ching* by Laozi:

Hesitant, like crossing a river in winter—
Cautious, like fearing four neighbors.

In contemporary Western culture, which has become the dominant model for much of the world, anxiety is often seen as a condition that can be treated in specific ways, partly through therapy and partly through medication. This is a relatively new way of trying to deal with anxiety.

In the older, classical Chinese model of health care, anxiety is seen to be part of a person's overall energetic pattern. Thus, the well-being of the whole person is what is studied and strengthened. The qigong tradition of cultivating internal energy is devoted to this approach. "Qi" means "energy"; "gong" means "work."

Some practitioners believe these two approaches are poles apart. In fact, they can be bridged. There is nothing in this book that requires anyone to give up whatever medication, therapy, or self-help methods they are using to cope with their anxiety. Also, the energy work offered in this book can be used whether you have a diagnosed anxiety disorder or simply struggle with varying levels of day-to-day anxiety.

Qigong does not treat your feelings—even your most fearful and difficult feelings—as enemies. This centuries-old tradition is based on respecting a person's feelings, attitudes, and behaviors—including their deepest psychological patterns—as part of their total energy field. Working with that total field of energy, rather than splitting it up, is at the heart of this system of well-being.

This is where ancient wisdom and the most contemporary scientific studies meet. Both focus on the totality of being. Both emphasize the reality of each person's direct, personal experience. The practice of qigong presented in this workbook is completely compatible with those therapeutic practices that empower individuals to relate with physical and emotional pain in ways that see these as powerful aspects of living a full life.

Interestingly, the word "anxiety" in the English language comes from a root word meaning "I cannot breathe" or "I'm choking." One of the translations for the Chinese word "qi" is "breath." Often, people having a panic attack are told to take several deep breaths. Imagine what it would be like if we were able to breathe in that relaxed, calming way each moment of our lives.

Human Being

In classical Chinese, a single character of two strokes is sometimes used to represent a person. This is the uppermost of these two characters. It represents a person walking. Encoded within these two brushstrokes is the deep understanding that life is a process. It is always in motion. It is always changing. It is always shifting, in the same way that our weight moves from foot to foot. Whenever we see this character, it tells us that life is moving forward.

Below it is the character for "body." Taken together, these two ideograms express the notion of "human being." In the classical Chinese tradition, it is considered a rare and precious opportunity to be born as a human and have both a human mind and a human body. We believe this potential is a gift. It gives us the ability to accomplish many wonderful things. Whatever storms we encounter, whatever difficulties we face, we believe we should make the best possible use of this extraordinary opportunity.

Understanding Your Energy Field

Every human being is a field of energy. Energy doesn't simply flow through us—we *are* energy. This was discovered by humanity's earliest natural scientists—the ancient Chinese physicians who studied the mysteries of the human body and mind. It has also been discovered by the modern scientists who reveal the wonders of our subatomic existence.

Whatever we experience occurs within that field of energy. Whether we experience anxiety, fear, and pain or deep well-being, joy, and freedom from pain, it is all an experience of energy.

In classical Chinese medicine—humanity's oldest continuous tradition of health care—one of the principal causes of pain and dysfunction is tension. We tend to think of anxiety and tension as a problem of mental well-being, but to the earliest Chinese physicians, mind and body were so intimately connected that mental tension could be locked into the body at its most subtle level.

Their findings have been validated by modern neurological research. We now know that tension shows up at the cellular level, obstructing the flow of oxygen and other nutrients, as well as preventing the elimination of dead or infected organisms. The inevitable result of anxiety and tension is pain, disorder, and disease.

Inner Relaxation

Inner relaxation is therefore not a luxury. It is the key to health. Understanding this, China's earliest natural scientists and medical practitioners worked patiently to discover systems of health care that would reduce the effects of anxiety and promote inner healing.

References to these systems appear in the oldest and possibly most influential text in the history of medicine, *The Yellow Emperor's Classic of Internal Medicine*. It dates back more than two thousand years, and its wisdom certainly goes back even farther than that. It includes an early reference to the system of cultivating energy described in this book: the practice of "standing still without changing" originally described by the Taoist master Laozi. *The Yellow Emperor's Classic*, which was written much later, includes this passage:

> The Emperor Huang Ti said:
>
> > I have heard that in ancient times there were Spiritual Beings. Their knowledge was vast and their understanding was profound.
> > They stood between heaven and earth, connecting the universe;
> > They understood and were able to control both yin and yang, the two fundamental principles of nature.
> > They inhaled the vital essence of life;
> > They remained unmoving in their spirit;
> > Their muscles and flesh were as one.
> > This is the Tao, the Way, which you are seeking.

This describes the essence of the mind-body practices in this book, the way in which apparently simple positions and gestures regulate the flow of life-giving energy that circulates within and around the human body and its nervous system at all times.

My own master in Beijing, Professor Yu Yongnian (pronounced "Yoo Yongnyan"), who died at the age of ninety-four while this book was in production, was fond of the writings of Laozi and liked to quote that passage from the Yellow Emperor. Talking to me about what it feels like to do these mind-body practices, he once said, "As you stand, you breathe in not only the air, but the vital essence of life, real energy. Real energy is what you are inhaling."

Our Energy Flow

There is an interesting relationship between the impact of this type of exercise on our physiology and its effect on our nervous system. Tests show that qigong has a deep, calming effect, while heightening our alertness. Practitioners of qigong tend to breathe more deeply, resulting in increased oxygen consumption. Their heart rate is slower but more powerful, resulting in increased stroke volume. They test well for alertness, but with negligible muscle tension. Those who regularly practice this type of exercise can attest to their improved powers of concentration, coordination, and inner balance.

Seen through the lens of the qigong tradition, these are all signs of the unobstructed flow of the energy that enables life to flourish. If the flow of energy is blocked, then, like stagnant water, energy putrefies. What blocks the flow of qi within our bodies is tension—the subtle effect of mental strain on our muscles and nerves. Qigong practice relieves this tension and clears the blockages.

With the blockages cleared, the heightened flow of energy automatically strengthens and calms our nervous system, because this inner relaxation and power is our natural state. What many people call a "normal life" is, in fact, the anxiety and discomfort we experience as a result of living with diminished and obstructed energy.

A very low level of energy leaves us feeling drained of vitality, but we are also susceptible to short rushes of intense energy. We feel unstable. We often wake up feeling like we haven't slept. We feel hassled by family life and work. Sometimes we push ourselves late into the night. Underneath it all is constant anxiety. We feel vulnerable, often protecting ourselves with aggression toward others. It is almost like the vulnerability we experience if our immune system is weakened. Our emotional life shows the same patterns. We are vulnerable to inner turbulence. We are susceptible to panic and despair. All of this is the effect of weak, unreliable energy.

Although you may recognize some aspects of that picture in yourself, it is probably not an accurate portrait. Your energy level is probably not that low. Much of the time you probably function well and feel fit. But since you are interested in this book, there are probably some days when you have an underlying sense that all is not well. You may feel that your energy fluctuates and that sometimes you lack stamina. You may be easily irritated at times, stressed and upset. This points to a level of energy that, while manageable at times, is irregular at others. It might be like a stream making its way through difficult terrain. It can be blocked by sudden shifts in the landscape or debris. On an emotional level, you may at times feel overwhelmed, frustrated, and agitated.

A fuller and more stable energy flow is less likely to be obstructed. Like a river, the current is constantly flowing. We have greater staying power and are more resilient. We still experience the full range of emotions—in fact, we are likely to be even more alive in our emotional life—but the ups and downs of anxiety, fear, and other agitated states do not overwhelm us. They are part of the current. Opening up to that experience and raising your natural energy to that level is the possibility that this book offers you.

The Qigong Workbook for Anxiety

Natural Growth

All authentic growth takes time. So does healing and the process of deep strengthening. It is like giving birth.

In the more than thirty years that I have been teaching these arts and treating people in the West, I have always had to tell people that nature takes time to form, nourish, and give birth to new life. I tell my students, "You can't make a plant grow by tugging on it every day. You simply put it in good soil, give it just enough water and light, and let it grow. If you do that, it will grow naturally. That is its nature."

We are all living at a time in history when the world seems to have sped up a lot, and there is a general expectation that everything can happen quickly, even overnight. So it's possible that some people have started reading and working with this book in the hope that it might quickly dispel all of the anxieties that they are having.

In my experience, some of the exercises and suggestions in this book can have almost immediate effects. That is not guaranteed, of course, because everyone is different, and the conditions in which people live and work vary widely. But even if you experience some immediate relief from the symptoms of your anxiety, that is not the point of this book—or the profound wisdom of the qigong tradition.

This book and the practice of qigong are about the cultivation and strengthening of the energetic core of your being. This is why my grand master, Wang Xiang Zhai (pronounced "Wang Shang Jai"; his story is told later, in the section "The Lineage"), told his students:

Preserving the heavenly wisdom, and maintaining the state of quiescence,
You are ready to act in response to all possible situations.

This energy work is hidden, unseen, and it takes place in the depth of your being. It is like the growth of a baby within a mother's body. Therefore, I suggest that you work with this book over a period of nine months, and in the opening and closing parts of this book, I have included charts you can use to pause and reflect on your overall experience of using the exercises over the course of that period. I hope this will help you care for and nurture deep, authentic growth within your being.

The next pages introduce you to some fundamental practices that will help you see the beneficial impact of apparently simple stretching, breathing, and calming exercises on your nervous system. Please don't be put off by their simplicity. They put you in touch with the deep simplicity and power of your own energy as a human being.

Coming Up for Air

"I'm drowning in it!" I hear people saying that all the time. They may be drowning in their work and the pressure of deadlines or in the overwhelming demands and conflicts in their lives. Or, like the student whose story I tell in part 3, "I Am Always Tired and Anxious," they might dream of themselves or others drowning. Such is the power that anxiety can exert over us. Just like someone who is sinking in water and running out of breath, we need to come up for air.

In the art of qigong there is a simple way to come up for air. You can do it sitting or standing; however, unless you are unable to stand, I recommend standing up to do this. So, if you are sitting as you read this page and really want to try coming up for air, stand up to do it.

It is best to stand with your feet shoulder-width apart. Now breathe in for a silent count of six seconds, opening your arms to your sides. Breathe in through your nose only, if you can.

As you are breathing in, your posture has the feeling of welcoming someone or being delighted to see an old friend coming toward you. Your palms are open. Look forward at the world.

Your chest naturally expands a little as your lungs fill with air and your arms open outward. You can see that when I do this, I bend backward very slightly and look upward a little. Please don't overdo this—do it just enough to experience the feeling of opening up and breathing in.

Sometimes, if you are very anxious or tense, your upper body, shoulders, and neck can feel stiff, so this movement could feel difficult the first few times you make it. This is natural—a sign of how much you will benefit from "coming up for air."

After breathing in for a silent count of six, breathe out, exhaling through your nose and mouth at the same time, and let your arms relax forward. It is good to feel your breath naturally leaving your torso through both your nose and mouth when you exhale. This clears stale air from your system and naturally enhances the depth of your next inhalation.

Your upper body relaxes so that you are very slightly bent over. Relax into this until you have exhaled completely. Your arms and hands hang loosely at your sides, possibly just a little forward, almost as if they are falling off. You feel a sense of natural release in your chest as your muscles relax. Your head can tilt a little forward too.

Coming up for air once is good. It can save the life of someone who is drowning. I recommend you do this six times, without rushing through it.

There is no need to hold the breath or exaggerate the movement. This is a very natural and subtle way of changing the energetic pattern of your being, right on the spot. See the effect for yourself.

"I Have Always Been a Worrier"

One of my students is an accountant. When he first came to see me, he was clearly worried about something. I didn't ask him about that, however, and he simply joined my classes and started learning qigong.

As I got to know him better, he opened up a bit. He told me, "I have always been a worrier. I found out some time ago that often the things that I worried about were quite trivial. But they consumed most of my mind. My worrying often hampered me from doing something about the actual problem. The only break I had from this cycle of worry was when I went to work, where I had other responsibilities placed on me, like meeting deadlines or producing accounts to a deadline. But then I worried about them as well."

It seemed from what he told me that he worried about almost everything in his life. One day he told me that the things that worried him stretched from problems with his car to concerns about his own health and the health of his family. But, he told me, things had started to change.

"Once I started doing qigong, things began to change," he said. "While I was standing without moving, I began to see that the thoughts that were causing me anxiety were like a broken record. They just went round and round. I soon realized that I could quite easily have other thoughts. I could think about good times and places. This had a profound effect on me. After my qigong practice, I felt the things that were troubling me were not as insurmountable. In fact, they often seemed insignificant. When I was practicing qigong, I was a different person—without all the problems."

There was a period of time when I didn't see him much. I found out that there had been a serious illness in his family. His sister had been diagnosed with pancreatic cancer and was given eighteen months to live. "My qigong practice was particularly useful then," he told me. "I used to see her every day. My daily qigong practice helped me stop worrying about her and accept the reality of the situation. That helped me, and I think it helped everyone else."

He said, "This is how I look at situations now. If they cause me concern and I can do something about them, then, of course, I do what I can. Otherwise, I am able to accept what is happening."

Sitting Up

The energy patterns we associate with anxiety have several forms. They can shift from one to the other, creating whirlpools of energy that leave us often feeling quite scattered. When people get to this state, they often say, "I need to collect myself." Whether you are feeling that or not, it is always helpful to gather your energy. It naturally reorganizes itself if it has a chance to settle—even for a short time.

Sitting up, in the midst of everything, for a minute or so is one way to do this. It is simple but extremely powerful. Anxiety and anxiety-related energy patterns often cause energy to get disturbed and blocked in the upper body and head. This contributes to confusion, increased tension, and headaches. The simple practice of sitting up helps move that energy lower in the body, where it can be more naturally rebalanced. As you can see from the relaxed position shown here, you do not need to hold yourself in a rigid position.

If possible, sit on a chair that supports your back, which will enable energy to flow freely and relieve your torso and inner organs of pressure. Since the spinal cord runs between the brain and the base of the spine, having your back supported and relaxed helps the flow of energy.

The difference between simply straightening the spine for a minute and the qigong practice you are going to do here is that you will hold this relaxed, upright position for between one and two minutes.

You breathe naturally while sitting up. Your eyes are open, although you can half-close them if you wish. Your hands can rest anywhere. To begin with, you are simply straightening the spine in a simple, natural way and remaining in that position for a short period of time.

You can think anything you want. Do not try to constrain the natural movement of the mind—that only increases tension.

After you have practiced the first stage of sitting up, the next stage is to sit with your ankles crossed. Some people find this more comfortable, and you can feel that it produces a different sensation in your lower body and abdomen.

Although you will have your feet flat on the floor again in the third stage, this intermediate step is very helpful for lower body relaxation and for helping you settle into the sitting posture.

Keep your spine as upright and relaxed as possible, without strain. You can relax your chest with the following simple method. First, breathe in deeply, and then breathe out through your nose. Don't force the air out, but exhale as fully as possible. As you do this, let your chest sink down a little. Your shoulders will drop a little. After this first complete breath, breathe naturally. Your hands can rest loosely in your lap, on your thighs, or in any position that is comfortable.

This is a moment of simply sitting still. It provides a healthy pause in your day and is part of the subtle process of cultivating your natural energy. When you feel ready, move on to the third stage.

If you are comfortable with the previous two sitting postures, you can try this slightly more advanced stage. You might be tempted to go straight to this posture; you can, but I recommend following the three stages of sitting up. To some people, these subtle adjustments may seem like nothing at all. It can be hard to understand why they are important.

In this third position, your knees are wider apart. This improves the flow of energy throughout the whole body and from the earth up into the body (earth energy is stabilizing).

Your open hands rest comfortably on your thighs. This helps relax your hands, arms, and upper body, which improves the flow of energy from your head, through your torso, and to your lower body and back. Your eyes are open or half-closed.

Sitting like this for a minute or two, up to a maximum of five minutes, is very helpful for stabilizing your energy.

Do not confuse this practice with any form of meditation. You are not asked to concentrate on anything, to breathe in any particular way, to stop thinking, or to do anything in particular with your thoughts or emotions. If you feel anxious while doing this, please just allow that to happen while sitting in this relaxed way. This, in itself, is strengthening and stabilizing for your energy. Your anxiety will learn to trust that.

If you are feeling particularly anxious, you can place a glass of water (preferably one made of green or blue glass) on a low table slightly in front of you and gaze gently at that. Further suggestions about the use of water in this kind of exercise are included in the practice "Looking into a Glass of Water" in part 4.

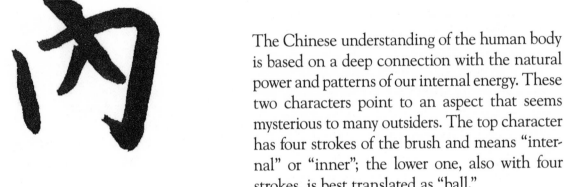

The Golden Ball

The Chinese understanding of the human body is based on a deep connection with the natural power and patterns of our internal energy. These two characters point to an aspect that seems mysterious to many outsiders. The top character has four strokes of the brush and means "internal" or "inner"; the lower one, also with four strokes, is best translated as "ball."

In the Taoist tradition, this is known as the "golden ball." "Golden" here means "not easy to find." It is rich. It is rare. The golden ball is also sometimes known as the "dragon ball."

The golden ball is one of the main fields of study for qigong masters and students. It develops within us as we cultivate our inner strength. As we work with the golden ball, our nervous system is strengthened until it is able to embrace all disturbances, including anxiety, shock, and fear.

The Golden Ball

There are several ways you can imagine the golden ball, all of which are part of the mind-body work of the qigong tradition. One way is to imagine that your body is surrounded by a sphere of golden light. This sounds fanciful, but this ancient, poetic idea expresses a phenomenon that you can now test with technology that measures the strength of your aura—the energetic field of the human body that extends slightly beyond the surface of the skin. We experience an aspect of this energetic "glow" when we feel the heat of a person next to us, even when he or she is not actually touching us.

There are other energetic patterns that the qigong tradition refers to when speaking about the golden ball. For example, there is a very strong concentration of energy in the lower abdomen, below the belly button. In classical Chinese medicine, this is known as the *dantien (tan tien)*, pronounced "dan dyen." It is sometimes called the "sea of qi," but is more literally translated as the "field of elixir." This can be thought of as a golden ball. A skilled practitioner learns how to develop the energy of this golden ball and can do this both internally and externally.

The stronger the energy field of the golden ball in your dantien, the higher the overall energy level of your whole being. A higher energy level is capable of accommodating a wide variation of energy patterns associated with our physical, mental, and emotional states. Our energy becomes like a great river, with many currents and countercurrents borne along with its flow.

One way of working with the golden ball is to imagine that it is a physical ball—light, like a balloon, or heavy, like a bowling ball—that we hold in a relaxed way between our open hands. We can hold it and move it as if it were actually there. After a while, it surprises many people to find that they are starting to feel the presence of energy between their palms. Not everyone feels it right away, of course—everyone's experience is different. "What's that?" people ask me, when they start to feel their hands tingling a little, and they are worried that their imagination is getting the better of them. "It's your golden ball," I tell them.

Resting the Golden Ball

You can practice resting the golden ball in your lap while sitting. This adds power to the stabilizing benefit of the sitting practice you did earlier, "Sitting Up."

Sit comfortably and be aware of your body weight resting on a chair or stool. Rest your back against the chair to support your spine. Let the muscles of your torso relax. Let your arms hang loosely by your sides. This will help you drop and relax your shoulders.

Slowly spread your elbows, moving them away from your body, as if small balloons were inflating between your elbows and your sides.

Then slowly move your hands in front of your lower abdomen, as if gently taking hold of a large golden ball in front of your belly.

It is extremely important to keep your chest completely relaxed as you do this. Do not struggle to hold your arms up with the muscles of your upper torso. Your elbows and shoulders are completely relaxed as you hold the ball in front of your belly.

Then lower your hands so that the backs of your hands rest lightly on your thighs, so the golden ball is gently resting in your lap.

Try not to lower your head, either to look down or because the relaxation of your shoulders makes you lean forward. Remain relaxed, looking forward. Breathe naturally.

As you imagine your hands holding the golden ball, your palms and fingers naturally develop a soft curve, as if molding themselves to the surface of the large ball. Your fingers are not held tightly together; they are gently separated, spreading across the surface of the golden ball.

Keep your chest and shoulders relaxed to avoid any strain in your upper body. Your qi will flow more freely if your upper body is relaxed.

Sometimes when people start to relax like this, they have a tendency to let their hands and fingers droop and to close their eyes. Please try to remain in the original position, even if you feel a little drowsy.

Your eyes are open or half-closed. If you don't feel like looking straight ahead, you can let your gaze rest on the floor about six feet in front of you.

You are holding the golden ball in your lap all this time. This means that your palms and fingers are in place, gently open and curved along the surface of the ball. Do not close them too much (as if holding a baseball or an egg) or open them too much (so much that a large ball would roll off your lap). This subtle work with the golden ball helps the overall circulation of energy in your body, settling any disturbances in its flow.

"Worrying About the Person in the White Coat"

You might be asking yourself if it is possible that simply sitting still and resting an imaginary golden ball on your lap could actually have an effect on your anxiety. One of my senior students recently shared with me an account of the usefulness of "Resting the Golden Ball." She used to work as a nurse in a major London hospital and now leads qigong classes for older people.

"It's well-known that people get anxious when they visit a health professional," she told me. "They start worrying about the person in the white coat. They might have worrying symptoms. They may be going to receive test results and are fearful about the diagnosis. Even if they are going for a routine check, they may be worried that they won't pass it."

She told me that one of her students had experienced this kind of anxiety. She was eighty-five years old and had managed to remain healthy, active, and independent. But in the last year, her husband had died, and one of her daughters had moved to Australia. So she was experiencing major changes in her life. The last thing she wanted to have at that point was a health problem. But she was diagnosed with high blood pressure and was asked to come back for a further test. My student told me what happened:

> I could see she was visibly worried. I reminded her that the qigong postures she was learning in class could be done sitting down and could help relax her. At the next class, she reported back to me. While sitting in the waiting room, she decided to put her qigong training to the test. She sat up comfortably, placing her feet flat on the floor. Without making a fuss, she practiced "Resting the Golden Ball." She held her hands in front of her belly, holding the invisible ball, with her hands gently positioned on her thighs. She decided to stay like that until she was called in for her appointment.
>
> When she eventually went in to see the doctor, she felt told me she felt remarkably relaxed and calm. She had her blood pressure test—it was lower than it had ever been on any of her previous visits. The medical professionals were extremely surprised, and, as you can imagine, she was delighted. Now she tells me she is doing the seated posture whenever she feels anxious—and she is feeling much more relaxed about everything, including going back to the doctor.

Rolling the Golden Ball

Having rested the golden ball on your lap for a little while, you can now advance to the next energy practice.

Lift the golden ball up, and hold it in front of your chest for a moment. Then slowly move the golden ball upward and away from your chest—outward—in a gentle curve. Complete the circle by bringing the ball down and in toward your belly.

Keep your elbows loosely bent, so they move naturally with the movement of your hands. Breathe out as the large ball circles up and outward. Breathe in as the ball comes down and in toward your belly.

As you roll the ball away from you and breathe out, imagine your energy is sending away any anxiety, pain, and other difficulties. You are using the movement and your mental intention to create a flow of energy that unblocks and releases the inhibiting patterns created by fear, anxiety, and uneasiness. This motion feels steady and full, strong and heavy.

If you can, make at least a dozen circles with the golden ball.

"Several Hundred Peanuts"

When I was a young man, I wanted to join the police. This was in Hong Kong when it was still under British rule; the police force was known as the Royal Hong Kong Constabulary. To be accepted, I first had to graduate from the cadet college.

One day, when I was going about my duties at the cadet college, my commanding officer came up to me, very angry with me. He accused me of something I hadn't done, which made me extremely upset. Because I didn't apologize, he threatened to dismiss me. It was nearly the end of my dream of joining the police. Luckily, he let me off with a warning.

I was furious. I had been wrongly accused, but if I had talked back, I would certainly have been kicked out of the college. I went to see my master, from whom I was learning martial arts. He was in his eighties and was a very great teacher. I told him my story and asked him what to do. I was angry, because I felt I would now be on a list of badly behaved cadets in the college.

Much to my amazement, after listening to me, my master gave me a sack of unshelled peanuts. He told me to sit down and start throwing them into a huge pot some distance in front of me. "Throw your anger away," he said. "Then I'll tell you what to do."

There must have been several hundred peanuts in the sack. When I had thrown them all into the pot, he made me tea. Then he asked me, "What do you think you should do?"

For a moment, my mind was blank. I didn't know what he was talking about, and when he reminded me, the incident no longer seemed to bother me. He had used my body to calm my mind.

Your Inner Reservoir

Our internal energy naturally gathers in a reservoir deep inside our lower abdomens. As we go about our busy lives, most of us are unaware of this inner source of strength, and it can become depleted. When that happens, we can feel anxious.

Qigong gives you a way of replenishing your energy, as well as developing your inner reservoir and preparing it for fresh energy. I recommend that you do this practice after any of the previous exercises. It is also helpful at any time, no matter what you are doing. It is a wonderfully calming exercise that soothes your nerves and restores your energy.

With a relaxed, slow motion, bring your right hand to rest over your lower abdomen. Rest your entire palm and fingers there, just below your navel.

Then slowly bring your left hand to rest on top of your right hand. Rest your entire palm and fingers on the back of your right hand.

It's important to make this movement slowly, and to try to avoid hunching your shoulders or tensing your chest. Otherwise there will still be some tension in your upper body. You can prevent this by first letting your arms hang loosely by your sides, then slowly moving your forearms and hands up toward your belly without raising your elbows.

Feel the sensations in your belly and hands as you sit still. Your hands are calm over your belly. Breathe naturally.

Rest like this for a minute.

Your Experience, Day or Night

You have now been introduced to several exercises that you can experiment with at any time of the day or night, whenever you are feeling anxious, or when you just want to take a break or refresh your energy. You can use the following chart to make notes on your experience. There are no right or wrong experiences; everyone's sensations are different. Sometimes you feel no sensations at all. It might be useful to review your responses in the chart "A Quick Check" at the end of the introduction. If you find this helpful, you can continue to keep notes for yourself on a separate notepad.

	If you have tried this exercise, what was your initial experience of doing it?	If you have continued to work with this exercise, what effects are you noticing?
"Coming Up for Air"		
"Sitting Up"		
"Resting the Golden Ball"		
"Rolling the Golden Ball"		
"Your Inner Reservoir"		

Wu Ji

It takes many strokes of the brush to write these two ancient characters, yet they represent the deepest simplicity of the universe. Their meaning is mysterious and hard to fathom, but they also are the name of one of the most practical of all exercises in the world of qigong.

The phrase is "wu ji," pronounced "woo chee" (and sometimes spelled "wu qi"). "Wu"—the upper character—symbolizes what exists before anything emerges from nonexistence. Just like the clear and infinite sky that can give birth to endless clouds and abundant rain.

Beneath it is "ji," which means "end." Not "end" in the sense of "final" but in the sense of that which is never reached. Taken together, these two timeless characters are symbols for an endless circle that contains and gives birth to everything.

Wu Ji: The Position of Primal Energy

There are said to be thousands of styles of qigong. All are forms of internal energy work. Some involve elegant and graceful movements. Some are based on the movements of animals and birds. All aim to cultivate the energy of the human being, and some of them also teach the practitioner how to work with the energy of the universe around us.

Among these thousands of possibilities—handed down from parents to children over the centuries, and secretly from masters to their students—there is one method that is distinguished from the rest, *zhan zhuang* qigong (pronounced "jam jong chee gung"). It literally means "standing like a tree energy work." It is famed for its most remarkable characteristic: it involves no movement.

This is the mysterious practice described in the verses of the *Tao Te Ching*, one of humanity's greatest literary treasures (and said to be one of the most widely translated texts in history).

Standing alone and unchanging,
One can observe every mystery,
Present at every moment and ceaselessly continuing—
This is the gateway to indescribable miracles.

My late master, Professor Yu Yongnian, whose story is told later in "The Lineage," was the world's leading authority on zhan zhuang qigong. In a lecture in London in 1998—on one of his rare trips outside China—Professor Yu said:

The history of health care in China stretches back into the distant past. As elsewhere in the Far East, a tradition has developed of taking care of one's own body and mind….In the West, although material life has developed enormously, there has not been a corresponding development in taking care of the human being. As a result, in today's society, people face enormous pressures both at work and at home. These create depression and many other mental and emotional difficulties. What people need is a way of looking after themselves, a way of taking care of their mental and physical well-being. What is needed is a method of self-healing….What is real relaxation? How would we know how to do that? Simply sleeping is not full relaxation. Nor is normal exercise, which deals almost entirely with our muscles. What is needed is a method of looking after ourselves that also relaxes our minds at the same time.

That method is the system that Professor Yu taught me—zhan zhuang qigong, "Standing Like a Tree."

The fundamental practice of wu ji is to align yourself, normally in a standing position, so that your body is centered, well-balanced, and upright—and to remain in that position, without moving, while you progressively relax all your muscle groups, until the flow of energy within you and around you gives you what might be called a complete energy bath. In the following pages, you are introduced to the opening phases of practicing wu ji.

In my experience, this is a wonderful practice for both calming and strengthening the nervous system. Students of mine who have experienced high levels of anxiety, panic, and fear have found that this ancient—and apparently simple—practice transformed their experience. I have included a number of their stories throughout this book.

Almost nothing seems more natural than simply standing still, but not everyone can do this, strange as that might seem. We might be familiar with the military posture of standing at attention, but that does not normally have an internal relaxation practice associated with it. There is also postural adjustment that normally takes place when people practice wu ji. It can take time to see clearly what adjustments might be needed and then to allow them to take place naturally as you stand in the position. Some people also find standing still very startling, since there is normally so much commotion in their lives. For these reasons, I would like to take you through a step-by-step approach to wu ji, which will begin in this first part of the book and will deepen later.

Starting Wu Ji

To begin your practice of wu ji, you will be using a wall or something similar to support your back and help you relax. Many people unconsciously hold a lot of tension in their

upper body musculature, because of the stress and anxiety in their lives. So using a support at the base of the spine will make a big difference in the depth of your relaxation.

Find something solid to lean against, such as a wall. In the kitchen, you can stand with your lower back against the fridge or a counter. Or you may have a piece of furniture that works well for you.

Stand with your feet shoulder-width apart. Rest your backside gently against the wall or other support behind you.

Your shoulders and chest are relaxed. Your breathing is natural. Stand still, fully at rest with your eyes open.

Your feet take the weight of your body, like the base of a great pyramid, and the wall or counter you are leaning against stabilizes you.

This photo shows the position from the front. Your arms are loosely relaxed by your sides.

At this stage in your practice, you are still resting your backside against a support. You may feel that you are tilted slightly forward as a result of doing this, particularly if you're using a wall as a support, but using the support for your back is helpful for the initial—and essential—inner relaxation process. Later you will progress to doing the full practice without the support, but at this stage it is important to become thoroughly familiar with the inner work without being distracted by instability in your back.

As you stand, please go through the progressive relaxation described just below, moving downward through your body.

Begin with a couple of minutes, if you can manage that. Then increase, day by day, until you are able to stand for five minutes or more, relaxed and motionless.

Calming Your Nervous System

Standing still in wu ji helps calm your nervous system. This process of relaxation is vital to your health and well-being. If your nervous system is agitated, the flow of energy throughout your body is seriously impeded. As you stand in wu ji, follow the following inner relaxation sequence.

Inner relaxation is the secret of all health and well-being. As you practice the postures and movements in this book, your inner work is to relax—whether you are standing still or moving. You can then carry this inner relaxation with you throughout your day, whatever you are doing.

Inner Release

Bring your attention to the area of your eyes. Release any tension you may be holding in the skin or muscles. If your eyes feel tired, imagine you are releasing the pressure in your eyeballs. Then bring your attention to your jaw and make sure you are not clenching your teeth. Relax your tongue.

Let this sense of relaxation flow down your neck and over your shoulders. Allow each shoulder to sink, releasing any tightness. Your arms will naturally drop slightly as your relax. Release tension in your chest by breathing out gently.

Imagine you are standing under a warm shower. As the water cascades down your back, feel it washing away any tension in your back, as if dried mud were being softened and washed away by the water. Feel the weight of your body sinking down through the soles of your feet.

Finally, imagine a fine golden cord supporting you from the top of your head. It stretches up into the heavens, gently suspending you. Remain still, repeating this inner relaxation as you stand.

"Like a Mountain with the Winds Howling Past"

One of my students is an independent management consultant. A few years ago he contracted pneumonia and lost more than twenty pounds in twelve days. He was off work for three months. But when he recovered and went back to work, he found he didn't have his earlier strength.

He has now been with me for several years and recently said, "My strength and immunity have increased to a level far better than average for my age. I had a weak lower back. This would often cause problems, including a very stiff upper back. Over the years, these have improved enormously....I genuinely feel as if, while I am getting older, my spine is getting younger."

I asked him about his internal energy and what effect it has on his high-pressure work in the business community.

He said, "Energetically, I have plenty of energy, focus, and sharpness. When it comes to anxiety, crises come and go. I went through a lengthy divorce. A company that went bankrupt owed me a great deal of money. It was an extremely difficult time for me. No one would choose to have those experiences. It has made a considerable difference to have some point every day when I could be like a mountain with the winds howling past—calm and unmoved. That tranquility in the eye of a storm has made a huge difference."

This student of mine also practices meditation. I asked him how he feels about qigong from that perspective. "The open-awareness of this qigong practice has allowed me to become more open and less self-orientated, as it were," he said. "There can be a huge divide between a state of calm you might experience in retreat and then your daily life. This divide does not arise the way we practice qigong. There is no split to be healed."

Standing and Rolling the Golden Ball

You were introduced earlier to the golden ball, including the exercise of rolling the golden ball while seated. Now that you have also been introduced to wu ji, you combine these two practices in this new exercise.

Begin by standing in wu ji. Imagine you are holding the golden ball in front of your chest, between your palms. Stand still for a moment before beginning the next movement.

Slowly circle the golden ball up and away from you, so that it moves in an arc outward, away from your chest. Complete the circle by lowering and bringing it in toward your belly. Keep your elbows loose, so that they move fluidly with the large circle of the golden ball.

Breathe out as the golden ball arcs up and outward. Breathe in as the ball comes down and in toward your abdomen. As you move the ball through the space in front of you, it feels strong and heavy.

Imagine that with each exhalation and outward arc of the ball, you are expelling any agitation and disturbing energy from your body.

Try making up to thirty circles with the golden ball.

Gathering Your Energy

This practice is an essential aspect of qigong exercise. It is a method of collecting your energy, directing it into its natural reservoir in the lower abdomen, and sealing it there. You can use it by itself, as a way of calming and centering your energy, or you can use it at the end of another exercise or a period of practice. It can also be used as an emergency treatment if you feel uncomfortable at any point in your qigong practice. In fact, you can use it as an on-the-spot method for getting some ground under your feet if you are overcome by strong emotion, experience intense pressure, or find yourself in a very difficult situation.

Stand with your feet shoulder-width apart. To begin, your arms are at your sides.

Open your hands and raise your arms out to the sides with your open palms facing forward. Continue to raise your arms until your hands start to come toward each other above your head. Breathe in as your arms circle up.

Bring your hands together so that of your right hand. This makes your arms into a complete circle, with your palms overlapped and facing downward. Your hands are directly over your head.

Then move your hands forward so that they are poised to come down in front of your face and upper body. Slowly lower your hands down in front of your body. You feel as if you are pressing a large ball down into water. Breathe out as your arms press down.

The movement continues until your palms are in front of your belly. You can let your hands gently slide down, touching your torso, if you wish.

Make three large circles like this, slowly and calmly.

Then calmly bring your palms to rest over your abdomen. Your right hand is against your belly, your left hand on top of it.

Rest in stillness, breathing naturally for a minute.

"To My Surprise"

Soon after we were married, my wife and I went from Hong Kong to London on our honeymoon. We planned to stay only a short time, but we have ended up living there for more than thirty years. Some of my earliest students are still coming to see me. One of them, a lawyer, held a senior position in a large legal department for a national professional body in the United Kingdom.

Just after he retired, he told me what he had been going through. "As the date of my retirement approached, I was waking up at four in the morning, worrying about the big changes in income and daily activity. I was often unable to get back to sleep."

This student is quite elegant and a real gentleman. He was honest about himself: "I am by temperament quite an anxious person. My fight-or-flight reaction has a low threshold and is easily triggered, causing mild panic and anxiety. This can be accompanied by thoughts of worst-case scenarios. They take on a life of their own."

I knew he was being honest with me when he spoke about his fears of retirement. "The accumulating sleep deficit and anxiety became self-perpetuating," he told me.

He wanted me to know what he did, because he had applied lessons he learned from studying qigong with me. "I found that if I got out of bed and stood in wu ji and then one other qigong posture for ten to fifteen minutes, my breathing became deeper and slower automatically. This led to a virtuous cycle, whereby my anxious thoughts and feelings diminished without any conscious effort on my part."

He said, "I had always thought that practicing qigong would make me feel wide awake. To my surprise, I found that on returning to bed, I felt calm and relaxed, and I fell asleep without much difficulty. I found the transition to retirement much easier than I feared—and I now have much more free time to practice qigong and enjoy life!"

Experiencing More Energy

In this part of the book, you have been introduced to the standing practice of wu ji and the progressive relaxation sequence that accompanies it. You have also learned standing and rolling the golden ball, and the practice of gathering your energy. These take you to a different level of energy work and have a more profound effect on your nervous system. You can use the following chart to make a note of your experience. It is all the more important at this stage to know that there are no right or wrong experiences; everyone's sensations are different. If you find these notes helpful, you can continue to keep notes for yourself on a separate notepad.

	If you have tried this exercise, what was your initial experience of doing it?	If you have continued to work with this exercise, what effects are you noticing?
"Starting Wu Ji"		
"Calming Your Nervous System"		
"Standing and Rolling the Golden Ball"		
"Gathering Your Energy"		

Inner Strength

These two Chinese characters stand for "inner strength." Literally, they mean "heart strength" or "experience held in the human heart." They express a feeling that is close to what we mean by "confidence," but they point to something deeper than that: not confidence in something, but confidence in anything.

For example, in the face of difficulty, you are not shocked. You do not feel helpless or worried. It is as if you have encountered this problem many times before and are thoroughly familiar with it. You already hold that experience in your heart. And not only are you familiar with this particular difficulty, but you also recollect what to do about it. Hence, you are able to draw on "experience held in the human heart." It is a hidden, personal treasure.

Inner Strength

"When I stand," said my grand master Wang Xiang Zhai, "the earth is in my hands. The universe is in my mind."

"You are free," he told his students. "You are a great fire. If anything comes toward you, it will be consumed in the fire. If it does not approach the fire, it will not be burned. You are merely the fire. You remain where you are, content to be alight."

"You are the sea," he told them. "Whatever anyone gives you, you can take. They can also take from you anything they want. The sea is vast; it can give up anything and still remain the sea. Like the sea, you are endless and unceasing. This is true freedom."

In Chinese culture, we have the tradition—which once also flourished in the West—of apprenticeship. Students learn from their masters by serving them; following their instructions; doing whatever is asked; and slowly, slowly being shaped by the wisdom and experience of the teachers. The teachers, in turn, are obliged to devote themselves wholeheartedly—for the sake of their art—to shaping the apprentices, and fashioning them into future masters. I have tried to keep that tradition alive, even though I am living in a very different culture now. Thus, I feel very happy to share with you these precious words of my grand master, hoping that you will grasp their profound meaning.

If you are suffering from tremendous anxiety and perhaps other emotions that overwhelm you at times, you might have turned to this book out of despair. I offer these words to you as a source of help. If you are willing to follow the simple instructions and practices in this book—to sit and stand, following the guidance I share with you—and perhaps, from time to time, to read the remarkable words of my grand master, then stamina, resilience, and great strength will naturally arise in your being. You cannot generate that strength through willpower and wishful thinking alone. But if you follow with care the practices in this book, you will be able, day by day, to create the fertile conditions in your body and mind that will make it possible for that inner strength to blossom within you, silently and beautifully.

Growing from Within—A Nine-Month Journey

Please take a few moments to reflect on your current experience. You will be using your answers here as a point of reference nine months from now, when you complete the "Inner Growth" worksheet at the end of this workbook. The purpose of these two charts is to help your inner development as you use this workbook and experiment with qigong. Please remember that every person is unique. There is no set pattern and no target. Qigong will help you ride the energy of all your experience. The following questions are meant for your personal, private use. Please treat them as an intimate conversation with yourself.

Date today:	Date nine months from now:

How does your anxiety show up in your life?
Are there any common patterns you see in the anxiety you feel at home, in your workplace, or elsewhere?
Do you have frequent sensations of fear or panic?
If you feel overwhelmed and have feelings of despair, how do you cope with them?
Anxiety is not always obvious to those around us. If your family and friends were asked if you suffered from anxiety, what do you think they would say?

Anxiety can affect our energy levels in different ways. How would you describe your normal energy patterns?

Anxiety can be tiring. Do you experience a lot of fatigue?

Anxiety can lead to physical tension. Do you experience tension in any particular part of your body?

Anxiety can contribute to sleeplessness. What is your normal pattern of sleep?

Do you wake up in the morning feeling anxious or in a bad mood?

Anxiety can contribute to digestive problems. Do you experience this? If so, in what ways?

On the basis of your experience with qigong so far, how would you like to use it to help you with your anxiety?

What is the main challenge you have faced so far in the qigong exercises you are practicing?

Frequently Asked Questions

Why does sitting and standing still in the various positions make you feel refreshed and energized? If it generates high levels of energy, why does it calm the nervous system?

These are questions I am often asked about qigong. The basis of understanding qigong is an appreciation of energy. From the earliest natural scientists of Chinese civilization down to the quantum physicists of our own era, there has been a tradition of understanding all phenomena as expressions of energy. In Chinese, this energy—or life force—is known as "qi." It is the basis of human life. It is none other than the vast force field that gives birth to and sustains everything in the universe—visible and invisible. The practice of qigong helps you feel this wonderful world of energy. You learn how to work with it and relax into it. It is like learning to float in a great river.

Do I need to follow a strict sequence of exercises?

No. Please feel free to experiment with the various exercises and suggestions in part 1. Everyone is different. Some people will make an immediate connection with an exercise; others won't. Some days you feel like trying one particular exercise; the next day you may not feel that way. There is a daily routine you can follow if you wish; you can find it in part 3. Many people like to add this routine to their day, since it only takes about ten minutes. But please feel free to make your own experiments with the practices and recommendations I am offering you.

What happens if I feel worse?

Sometimes when we start "Coming Up for Air" and begin letting go of accumulated tension, the mind and heart can start to race, like a wild horse let loose in a field. This is normal. If you feel it is too much, follow "Gathering Your Energy" in part 1.

I'm feeling good. Can I skip ahead?

Yes. This book is designed so that you can use it however you wish. It does not follow a strict, linear sequence. However, sometimes the very nature of anxiety keeps us skipping along, and we are unable to settle. Please notice this. When you find an exercise or a suggestion that you are attracted to, then please continue to do it regularly. You can add others as well, as additional experiments, slowly building up your repertoire. If you ever feel you are losing your way, come back to the very beginning and start "Coming Up for Air."

Opening Up, Relaxing, and Gathering Your Energy

Anxiety often makes us close up. We feel burdened, and we unconsciously constrict our muscles, particularly in the upper body. This puts pressure on our chests, and our breathing becomes shallow. That is why the very first qigong practice in this book is "Coming Up for Air." This starts the process of opening up.

As you stretch your arms back, your chest expands. Your lungs open. You take in more oxygen. At the same time, you are stretching your whole upper body. Then, as you come back to the resting position, with your arms hanging slightly forward, there is a natural relaxation. That feeling of relaxation is the key to deeper qigong practice.

Some people worry that they feel a little light-headed when they first start to do qigong exercises. This is *not* a sign of illness or that you are doing anything wrong. As your qigong practice deepens, you will naturally develop a much stronger connection with the energy of the earth. This literally grounds you. At first, however, as your internal energy wakes up, you might feel it floating upward. You might feel a little dizzy or nauseous, or you might have a sudden rush of emotion. In that case, please follow the exercise "Gathering Your Energy." This is what I call "Qigong First Aid."

Energy Field

These two characters express in Chinese what we call an "energy field." You will recognize the upper character as "qi," "energy." Underneath it is the character "qung" (pronounced "chung"), which represents an open space. It could be a football field, a large garden, or a great plain. It could simply be translated as "area" or "field." This space is not closed, like a room or a house. It is open. Because it is open, it can expand—it can grow. It can extend in all directions.

Every human being is an energy field. Our power, our capacity, and our potential are unbounded.

PART 2

Your Personal Energy Field

Health and Anxiety

Huge numbers of people are seeking a method of relaxation that will enable them to function effectively in their busy lives. They feel a persistent level of anxiety and tension in almost everything they do and almost everywhere they go. The times we are living through are sometimes referred to as "the age of anxiety." A student of mine showed me a magazine article that described people as "all jumpy and edgy and short of breath." It said that physicians write over ninety-four million prescriptions for antianxiety medication annually in the United States alone (Miller 2012). The *New York Times* recently featured a series of seventy essays on anxiety; the newspaper introduced the series by saying, "Nearly one in five Americans suffers from anxiety. For many it is not a disorder, but part of the human condition" ("Anxiety" 2013).

People who suffer from anxiety have a wide range of symptoms, including restlessness and a feeling of being constantly on edge. They get tired easily. They have difficulty concentrating; their minds go blank with worry. They are frequently irritated. They experience body pains from persistent tension in their muscles. They have difficulty falling asleep; their sleep is disturbed, with them often waking up in the middle of the night; and in the morning they wake up feeling that they haven't slept.

We tend to think of tension merely as a problem of mental attitude. But to the early Chinese physicians, mind and body were so intimately connected that mental tension could be locked into the body at its most subtle level. Their findings have been validated by modern neurological research. We now know that tension shows up at the cellular level, obstructing the flow of oxygen and other nutrients as well as preventing the elimination of dead or infected organisms. The inevitable result of tension is pain, disorder, and disease. Inner relaxation is therefore not a luxury. It is a key to health.

In the tradition of classical Chinese medicine, tension is one of the most common causes of pain and dysfunction. Tension blocks the flow of vital energy, qi, in the human body. When our qi is flowing smoothly and without obstruction, we experience health. When it is blocked or diminished, we experience pain and ill health. We also experience this pain and *dis*-ease in our attitudes, emotions, and thoughts. In fact, the two are so deeply interrelated as to be inseparable.

The exercises and practices in this book have been developed over many generations to balance muscular activity and relaxation so that your internal energy is strengthened. The overall effect on your nervous system and your mind is to calm you down, freeing you from debilitating anxiety.

The Benefits

Circulation is a key determinant of our health. If the flow of blood, lymph, and other fluids is restricted, the body begins to degenerate. Our tissue loses its softness, dries out, and becomes hard. Joints stiffen and muscles ache. Our immune system is weakened as the flow of immune cells in the intercellular fluid slows and is blocked.

Anxiety contributes to this degeneration. The many pressures of daily life put our whole system on constant alert, even in sleep. We see the results around us every day: hypertension, migraines, asthma, all manner of aches and pains, menstrual difficulties, depression, and heart attacks. We tend to store the effects of anxiety in our musculature—as everyone with a stiff neck knows.

The gentle movements and postures of qigong slowly alternate contraction and release of all the major pairs of flexor and extensor muscles, as well as many of the smaller, deeper muscles in the body that normally we rarely use. This work warms and massages your internal body tissue, thereby releasing and encouraging the flow of blood, lymph, and intercellular fluid.

The inner relaxation usually helps our posture. This is especially noticeable in older people who take up qigong after a period of relative inactivity. The spinal muscles elongate. The ligaments become more supple and the movement of the spinal column eases. From the point of view of the flow of vital energy within the body, this has a profoundly beneficial effect on the central nervous system and our consciousness.

Most people find that their breathing (which is easily affected and made shallow by anxiety) becomes deeper, slower, and more powerful as a result of qigong practice. Over time, I have noticed that their breathing rate can decrease from ten to twenty breaths per minute to six to eight per minute. Their breathing becomes smoother as their diaphragm becomes stronger. In hospitals in China, qigong has been used in the treatment of tuberculosis and chronic ailments such as bronchial asthma.

Digestive processes also benefit from qigong. Anxiety affects the digestive system, with frequent complaints including gastric pain, ulcers, and bowel problems. In some cases, people who had bowel movements only once every three days (or even less frequently) have reported having daily bowel movements after doing even basic qigong exercises.

My master, Professor Yu Yongnian, took an interest in the effect of qigong on the cardiovascular system. In one of his experiments at Ten Lu (Railway) Hospital in Beijing, he measured blood counts of qigong practitioners (using the system described in this book) before and after their daily practice. He found that their hemoglobin levels increased, as did their production of both white and red cells. Their blood protein levels also increased significantly, resulting in increased absorption of oxygen from the lungs and improved circulation of the oxygen-rich blood to the rest of the organs.

You might wonder what all this has to do with levels of anxiety and, more particularly, with reducing or getting rid of anxiety. An old Latin saying provides an answer: "A healthy mind in a healthy body." This was said, in good schools, to be the goal of educating the whole person. It also points to the interdependence between mind and body: the health of the body affects the health of the mind; the health of the mind affects the health of the body. Just take the example of Professor Yu's findings at his hospital. Imagine how our brain and nervous system would function if bathed in a nurturing flow of oxygen-rich blood. Wouldn't we feel alert, energized, and resilient? Imagine the contrast: the blood flow to the brain is constricted by muscular tension in the neck, and our shallow breathing means we have low levels of oxygen in our blood cells. Wouldn't this lead to reduced mental energy, increased worry, and a tendency to get stuck?

You may have tried many methods to lessen your anxiety. In the the following chart, you are asked, "If you are already trying to control your anxiety, what have you found most useful, and why do you think this has helped you?" It is useful to remind yourself of any methods that you have found useful, even if briefly. Nothing in this book counteracts any other method you might have found useful. You can practice these qigong exercises while receiving any other form of treatment or while using any other self-help method that offers relief from anxiety.

Using the Mind

The mind that is the anxious is same mind that can help us work with our anxiety. Our natural mental awareness is an ally. Although qigong may be different from other approaches you have tried, it has one important thing in common with most other methods: awareness. Your own awareness of what is happening to you makes a big difference in the effectiveness of what you do. Therefore, throughout this book there are charts to help you explore and keep track of your own experience.

Whether you have started using the qigong practices in part 1 already or are dipping into different parts of this book looking for help, you may find it helpful to review your own experience of your anxiety. If you completed "A Quick Check" at the end of the introduction, you may find that your answers there will help you think about your responses to the questions below.

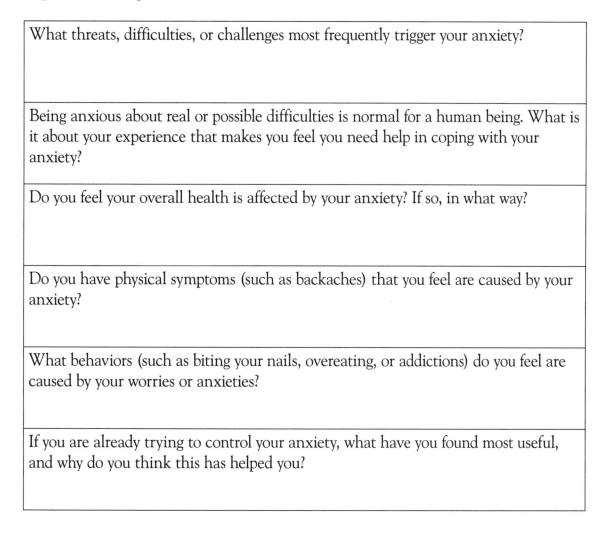

What threats, difficulties, or challenges most frequently trigger your anxiety?

Being anxious about real or possible difficulties is normal for a human being. What is it about your experience that makes you feel you need help in coping with your anxiety?

Do you feel your overall health is affected by your anxiety? If so, in what way?

Do you have physical symptoms (such as backaches) that you feel are caused by your anxiety?

What behaviors (such as biting your nails, overeating, or addictions) do you feel are caused by your worries or anxieties?

If you are already trying to control your anxiety, what have you found most useful, and why do you think this has helped you?

"You Need to Train Your Spirit"

When I was very young, my father allowed me to begin training with a master in our city, Hong Kong. This was my first experience of the wisdom and power that was later to become the subject of my life's work and study. I learned many important lessons about anxiety, tension, and relaxation. My training was based on the principle that physical and mental health was part of the same discipline of working with energy.

The fundamental rhythm of all energy fields is the interplay of yin and yang—the two interrelated energies in the famous Taoist symbol that weaves together light and dark. We need both energies to be whole, balanced, and healthy human beings, living a good life in the midst of the constantly shifting energies of human society and nature. Anxiety can be both yin and yang. Anxiety is yin when it undermines our ability to act. It is yang when it makes us frantic and tense. Like all energies, it can shift according to conditions. Qigong training cultivates the ability to work with yin and yang in all their forms.

The training I received from my master involved both yang and yin energies. First he taught me the martial arts. I learned some of the toughest forms, like those practiced by the famous Shaolin monks. One day I injured myself in a strenuous session. When I recovered, my master told me, "Now you must learn tai chi." This is the graceful system of slow, gentle movements, known worldwide. What he said upset me. I loved the speed and force of what he had trained me in already.

My master could sense my resistance. "You need to train your spirit," he said. My hard training had been developing my yang energy. Now I needed to cultivate my yin energy. During my years of teaching in the West, I have found that many people think that the gentleness of yin energy makes it weak. It is not. Indeed, in the *Tao Te Ching*, Laozi points out that water is more powerful than rock.

My master knew that I was becoming too tense. My spirit was hardening. He knew that I needed to cultivate another aspect of my being. Later, during my philosophical studies, I thought back to how he trained me and realized that he was instructing me in how to understand and work with yin and yang.

Holding On and Letting Go

Probably one of the most irritating things that anyone can say to an anxious person is "calm down," "relax," or "just let go." Not only do those statements almost always make the person feel worse, they are actually based on an inaccurate way of understanding how human beings function.

Being alive is a constant process of holding on and letting go. These are not opposite states; they are two aspects of the amazing, dynamic process of being alive. In every human being, this process takes place simultaneously, in some way, in every function of the body and mind. Think about your breathing, or your heart beating, or the process of digesting food and drink. Think about how you go to sleep and then wake, the way you walk, the many ways in which you communicate. All involve holding on and letting go, woven together in the intimate fabric of life.

So too with anxiety and all our emotions. They are part of this continuous, unfolding rhythm of life. Understanding this lies at the heart of the qigong tradition and is beautifully expressed in the *Tao Te Ching*.

Sometimes breathing is hard, sometimes it comes easily;
Sometimes there is strength, and sometimes weakness

This passage reminds us that disturbances of all kinds are part of life. They are episodic in nature and are not the whole of life. Another truth is hidden within these simple words. All turbulence arises and subsides naturally, through its own organic processes. This is as true for our emotional life as it is for the weather. This knowledge is embodied in qigong. Thus, I do not ask you to force yourself into any mental state or reject anything about your experience. Instead, I am offering you a way of fully embracing—even expanding—the fullness of your experience.

The exercises in the following pages enable you to embody this. Please experiment with them and then use the charts provided to track your own experience.

Arm Swinging

This simple movement releases the tension so often associated with anxiety, and it increases your flow of energy.

Stand with your feet pointing straight forward, shoulder-width apart. Look straight ahead. Make sure that your head is not slumped forward or tilted backward. Relax your shoulders and let your hands hang loosely by your sides.

Swing your arms loosely forward, with the backs of your hands facing forward, and your fingers gently spread apart. Let your hands swing up until they are level with your chest. Do not swing them higher than your shoulders.

Then swing your arms back until they naturally stop behind you. Keep them slightly away from your body. Do not bring your hands together behind your back; they should remain the same distance apart as when they were swinging forward.

Let the natural momentum of the swing carry your arms forward and then backward. Work toward a spontaneous and fluid swing. Build up to swinging your arms like this for up to three minutes, if you can.

What's Happening?

How can something so simple as swinging your arms help you with your anxiety? At first sight, it might seem impossible. That's especially true if you are someone who thinks that anxiety is a state of mind that has nothing to do with your body—and certainly not your arms!

But perhaps you also know that going to the gym or going for a run is good not only for your physical fitness but also for your mind. It can clear your mind and improve your overall mental stamina. Qigong works on the same principle, except that in qigong we are working with an even deeper, more subtle approach.

The way you stand in the arm-swinging exercise, with your feet flat on the ground and shoulder-width apart, is a traditional way of connecting with the energy of earth—the huge power source that nurtures all life on earth. Strong, sustaining energy comes up into our bodies through our contact with the earth. We know that intuitively when we go for a walk in nature or lie down on the grass.

When you begin to swing your arms loosely, several things start to happen naturally in your body. First, the gentle swinging encourages your shoulders, chest, and neck to relax. You can experiment with this by hunching your shoulders and tensing your neck and chest while swinging your arms. You'll immediately find out how difficult it is—you naturally want to loosen up. Loosening up these sensitive areas of the upper body is extremely important. It improves the flow of blood and lymph to and from the brain.

As your arms begin to swing, you feel sensations in your hands and fingers. Please try to keep your fingers open a little bit, so you can feel the air moving between them as they swing. This also helps encourage one the main effects of the swinging: the increased flow of blood all along the arms and hands, right through to the fingertips. That, in turn, stimulates increased circulation throughout the body.

How does that help with your anxiety? A combination of greater relaxation and increased blood circulation sends powerful signals to your whole nervous system. Anxiety often tenses and constricts your being, and with arm swinging, your body is sending the opposite signal to your nervous system—relax and open up.

From the classical Chinese point of view, there is also another reason. If you look at a chart of the meridians (energy pathways) that run through the body, you will see that all the main meridians have important terminal points in the hands and fingers. There's a saying in Chinese medicine: "the qi flows with the blood." So the increased circulation caused by the swinging is also stimulating the flow of qi throughout all the meridians, clearing stagnation and increasing the movement of energy.

Does it work better if you swing your arms higher and faster? No! Here is the difference between qigong practice and a tough workout in the gym. For energy to flow smoothly and powerfully in your body and to calm and rejuvenate your nervous system, relaxation is essential. So, hidden within this seemingly simple, ancient tradition is the potent combination of power and relaxation.

It may surprise you that arm swinging is widely used as a morning exercise in schools, factories, and businesses throughout China. It rouses people's energy and generally seems to put them in a good mood to start the day. Also, people seem to appreciate doing it with others. There is something about the simplicity and the rising energy of the exercise that feels good to share with a friend, your family, or a large group of schoolmates or colleagues.

Even more surprising to you, perhaps, is that this same exercise is used in traditional qigong hospitals in China for the treatment of serious illnesses, including some cancers, sometimes in conjunction with herbal treatments. In a hospital setting, arm swinging as a therapeutic treatment is done as a supervised exercise, since the patients devote themselves to the exercise for long periods of time.

The potency of the exercise lies in the subtle combination of the standing posture, which promotes a deep connection with the earth; the enhanced circulation of blood and qi caused by the arm swinging; and the inner relaxation, which releases internal blockages in the body's energy flow.

Please try it for yourself. There is a chart ahead to help you keep track of your experience at different times of the day and in different moods. Combining your exercise with the work of self-observation can deepen your own experience of this art.

"I No Longer Feel Tired"

One day a very charming lady came to see me at my clinic in London. She was middle aged and well dressed and had a dignified manner. It turned out that she was the head teacher of a good school in the city. I could tell immediately, from the way she walked, that she was suffering from postural pain. The way we hold our bodies is so often linked to anxiety.

"I have had this pain for years," she told me. "I have been to countless doctors. I have tried Western medicine, Eastern medicine, and all manner of alternative therapies."

In the Chinese medical tradition, particularly in the art of qigong healing, pain is almost always a sign that the natural flow of energy in the body is being blocked. The blockage and the pain may persist for years, but it does not necessarily take all that long to unblock the energy and restore its natural flow. Of course, it may take time to overcome the habit of tensing up, but in my experience, it is almost always possible to make a difference.

Here is where understanding the mind-body relationship is so important. Just as mental stress can produce tension and pain in the body, so too can we use bodywork to relieve the mind of its repetitive patterns of anxiety.

I asked my patient, the head teacher, to stand up and to swing her arms gently to and fro. She began, but within a few minutes I could see her habit of tensing up. Her shoulders were hunched, her elbows were not loose, and the swing was forced.

Years of caring, of being on constant alert, of helping others with their troubles—all wonderful human qualities—can have this effect on our nervous system if we are not careful. But because these patterns arise from a warm human heart, there is always a pathway back to a more natural state of being at ease, even in the midst of all the challenges we face.

I corrected her arm movements and let her continue swinging.

"Ah," she said suddenly after a few minutes, "I can feel it. I feel the relaxation in my tendons. They are no longer aching. My body feels comfortable."

I thought she would stop at that point. Much to my surprise, she kept on going. And then she smiled and said, "I no longer feel tired."

What Is Your Experience?

Part 2 introduces you to the apparently simple exercise of arm swinging. This is something that you are welcome to try at any time of the day or night, whenever you are feeling anxious or want to take a break, or if you want to refresh your energy. Many people are skeptical about the benefits of this exercise, because it seems too simple. How can something so easy, almost childlike, make a difference? There is only one way to find out: try it.

Please use the following chart to keep track of your experience. Everyone's sensations are different. Similarly, the effects can be different on different days and at different times of day. If you find this helpful, you can continue to keep notes for yourself on a separate notepad.

	What was your initial experience of swinging your arms?	If you have continued to work with this exercise, what effects are you noticing?
Early morning.		
During the day at work.		
Outdoors.		
While feeling anxious.		
While feeling tired.		

Opening the Curtains

Here is another apparently simple exercise that can help you in the midst of your anxiety. It is similar to the practice in part 1, "Coming Up for Air," but it has an even more powerful effect on your inner organs and nervous system. It is a quick way of overcoming the constricting effects of anxiety, nervousness, and fear, which can cause us to tighten up internally.

Stand with your feet pointing straight forward, shoulder-width apart.

Imagine you are about to open heavy curtains that are drawn closed in front of a large window in front of you.

Raise your hands to eye level, palms facing outward, as if placing them against the fabric of the heavy curtains. You are going to spread the curtains open, not pull them. Breathe in.

As you breathe out, use your open palms to spread the heavy curtains apart. Because they are heavy, you can't move them too quickly.

Open the curtains until your arms are out to your sides at around a forty-five-degree angle.

Once you are familiar with this motion, you can make it more powerful. As you open the curtains, lean forward a little to put some pressure on the balls of your feet. This presses on one of the most powerful acupuncture points in your body, the *yongquan (yung chuan)* point. It is a key power spot for your connection with the energy of the earth.

Then bring your hands back to the starting position. As you do this, stop leaning forward, stand flat on your feet, and breathe in. Repeat the movement three, six, or nine times. Then slowly lower your arms.

Your Opening Experience

"Opening the Curtains" works with the energy pathways that run from the *yongquan* point in the middle of each foot up to your fingertips. You many experience new sensations as you do this, and you may detect a change in your experience of anxiety or other disturbing emotions. You may find the following chart a helpful way to keep track of any effect this practice has on you, physically and mentally.

Please remember that these experiments are personal to you. If you find this exercise helpful and want to work with it over time, you can continue to keep notes for yourself on a separate notepad.

Is there any difference in your breathing before and after opening the curtains?
Do you notice any difference in how your head and neck feel?
Is there any difference in your vision or any difference in any sensations of pressure or discomfort in the area of your eyes?
Are your neck, chest, and upper back tense or relaxed? Have you noticed a change from doing this exercise?
How does your lower back feel before and after opening the curtains?
Does your body temperature change while you are opening the curtains?
As you practice opening the curtains, do you notice any shift in your attitudes, emotions, or thoughts?

"You Don't Know How Tense You Are"

One day my master said to me, "You don't know how tense you are." I was shocked and even a little resentful to hear him say that. I was a devoted student, still very youthful, doing my best to follow his instructions and training hard in the martial arts. A lot of the fast, repetitive exercises that have come down to us over the centuries, like swinging your arms rapidly in large circles, are designed to loosen up your joints and really free up your energy. We started our classes with vigorous warm-ups like this. The looser our joints, the more power in our punches. Even when we were sparring with our fellow students, our master would call out, over and over again, "Relax! Relax!"

On the day that he cautioned me about how tense I was, he came over and stood beside me and told me to do something new. "Clench your fists very tightly," he said, making his own hands into two tight fists. "Squeeze more tightly. Really squeeze hard. Now twist your fists in toward your body. Don't stop squeezing. Harder. Harder."

My fingers were getting sore from the pressure. The tendons in my forearms were really feeling the stretch. My wrists were starting to ache. My hands were getting hot. Then quietly he said, "Release." He opened his hands, and I opened mine.

I still remember the rush of energy. And I also remember that I was suddenly more relaxed than I had ever been. Oddly enough, he had showed me how to relax by asking me to tense up. Now I was learning that I could go much further than I had thought possible.

Tensing and Relaxing

You are now going to experiment with an approach to dealing with inner tension and anxiety that is patterned on the story "You Don't Know How Tense You Are." The point of that story and the point of this exercise is that we might be in such a state of constant muscular and nervous tension that we have forgotten what it feels like to be relaxed. We may think we are relaxing, but we don't know what that would really feel like. In this sequence we deliberately increase the tension in our arm muscles and then let go so that our nerves begin to experience the feeling of relaxation. The alternation helps our nervous system remember another way of being.

There are two forms of this method of tensing and relaxing that you will learn. The first one you will do while sitting or standing still. With the second, you will learn to add a powerful movement to it. Both forms involve a very powerful twist of both arms. You feel the effect coiling up both arms into your chest and shoulders, and you feel the corresponding release of tension as you uncoil.

Begin with your arms by your sides. Then gently bring your hands toward your abdomen, as if you are holding a large ball in front of your belly. Your elbows should be held away from your torso, allowing space under your arms. Relax your chest and shoulders. Breathe in.

Then rotate your forearms inward so that the backs of your hands face each other. Your palms are turned outward, facing away from the sides of your body. Your fingers are pointing away from you. Breathe out as you do this.

As your forearms turn inward, you may feel a slight twist in your upper arms. Pause for a second or two, holding this position, feeling the twist. You feel it coiling up your arms, into your chest and shoulders. Do not breathe for a second— wait to breathe in on the next movement.

Now, breathe in and let your arms return to the starting position, with your hands holding the imaginary ball in front of your belly. You feel the release of tension as you uncoil.

If you are doing this sitting down, you can rest your hands in your lap for a moment before doing the movement again. Breathe naturally for a moment. Repeat this sequence up to three times, if you wish.

Once you have become familiar with this exercise, you can add a further element. When you have twisted your forearms inward so that your palms are facing away from your body, squeeze your hands into fists as tightly as you can. Breathe in as you do this. Hold tight for a few seconds.

Then breathe out as you unclench your fists. Your forearms are still turned inward. Then, breathing in, let your arms return to the starting position, holding the imaginary ball in front of your chest.

Working with a Wall

Once you have tried "Tensing and Relaxing," you can add movement to it. You will be working with a wall, bouncing off it as you make the same twisting movements with your arms.

There are many different methods of tensing and relaxing, but they all work on the same principle. In the classical Chinese tradition, the alternation of tensing and relaxing is a perfect example of the powerful interaction between yin and yang. Tensing up involves yang energy—strong, focused, and hard. Relaxing involves yin energy—yielding, flexible, and soft.

In this exercise, the process of tensing and relaxing is rapid. It is a quick way of sending signals to the nervous system. The sudden and repeated interaction of yin and yang has the power to interrupt any patterns of anxiety, fear, panic, or obsession that may have taken hold of the mind.

To begin, stand with your back a few inches away from a wall. You will be bouncing your upper back against the wall, so check your position to make sure that you can do that. You can try rocking backward and forward on the soles of your feet to make sure you feel balanced and stable when your upper back touches the wall and when you lean a little forward. Most people need to be quite close to the wall to be able to do this.

Hold the large imaginary ball in front of your belly, as you did in "Tensing and Relaxing." Your elbows are held away from your torso, allowing space under your arms.

Now, let your body fall backward until your upper back bounces against the wall. As soon as your upper back touches the wall, there is a natural recoil that propels you forward away from the wall.

As you bounce forward, rotate your forearms inward so that the backs of your hands face each other, as you did in "Tensing and Relaxing." Breathe out as you bounce forward, twisting your arms.

When your body has come naturally forward, let your arms uncoil, so that you are holding the imaginary ball. Breathe in as you do this.

Repeat the movement three, six, or nine times. Do not exaggerate the movement. You are not slamming your back against the wall. You are bouncing with a natural rhythm.

As you become familiar with the movement, the exercise will be a natural process of rapid tensing and relaxing, synchronized with your breathing. Your breath will come in short, shallow bursts in time with the bouncing.

You can record your experience in the workbook charts. In particular, if you decide to do this exercise when you are feeling particularly anxious, try noticing your different states of mind before, during, and after this vigorous form of tensing and relaxing.

Clenching and Relaxing

Everyone reacts differently to qigong exercises. Some people find that a slower process of tensing and relaxing is more helpful than a rapid exercise. Please don't make the mistake of thinking that one method is better for your than the other. Don't worry that being able to do these exercises either faster or slower indicates something about your physical health or the state of your nerves. Each person is different. You need to experiment to see what works best for you.

Here is a slower method you can try, using your hands to clench and relax, synchronized with your breathing.

Sit or stand upright. This automatically releases pressure on your internal organs. Let your arms hang loosely by your sides for a second. Relax your shoulders.

Slowly open your elbows outward, away from your body. The movement is led from the elbows, keeping the shoulders still. Your arms rest in an open, relaxed curve on either side of your body.

Breathe in. Then make your hands into fists and clench them tightly while you hold your breath. Hold tightly for a few seconds.

Open your hands as you breathe out, and lower your hands to your sides. Breathe naturally. Repeat up to three times, if you wish.

Spreading and Relaxing

This exercise is the reverse of "Clenching and Relaxing." Here you spread your fingers wide apart, feeling the powerful stretch, and then let them relax.

Like all of these relaxation techniques, you can do this standing or sitting. If you work at a desk, this exercise can be easily adapted to your needs: you can conclude by resting your hands on your desk, rather than your lap, if that is more convenient for you.

Begin by raising your arms to chest level as if holding a large imaginary ball between your arms. Imagine the weight of your arms being supported by balloons under your arms.

Then turn your hands so that your thumbs point toward each other. Your palms face downward and your fingers point away from your body. Breathe in.

Then, as you breathe out, stretch your fingers and thumbs as wide apart as possible. The stretch should be as vigorous as possible, combined with a feeling that each finger is also extending forward.

Keep your fingers and thumbs spread apart for a few seconds, and hold your breath. Relax the spread and breathe out while gently lowering your hands to your lap or by your sides. Breathe naturally. Repeat up to three times if you wish.

"Locked Up in Anxiety"

Often, when people come to my classes or come to my clinic for treatment, one of the first things that I notice about them is that they are very tense. I can see the tension in their faces, the way they hold their bodies, and the way they move.

I usually give them some simple exercises to do. I tell them the movements are a warm-up, but actually, this is a way of trying to help them relax a little. Some of those exercises, like arm swinging, are in this book. But some people are so tense that even after these "warm-ups," their muscles are still tight. I used to tell them to relax, but that didn't work either. I realized that they had become so accustomed to being tense that they had no way of knowing how tense they actually were. They were literally locked up in anxiety.

I decided to try a method I learned from one of my masters. I asked them to tense up. For example, I would ask them to clench their fists until their knuckles went white. When I saw they could do this, I would tell them, "Squeeze harder; squeeze really tight!" They would put all their effort into this, even getting short of breath. When I saw they couldn't stand it any longer, suddenly I would tell them to relax and breathe out.

I could see the look in their eyes. The contrast between the extreme clenching of the fists and the sudden release of that tension gave them an experience they had not had for years. In that moment, they caught a glimpse of what it might be like to relax.

Not only did they begin to let go of tension in their bodies, but that physical sensation began to affect their minds. Their minds were following their bodies. They could feel inner pressure being released. The process of tensing and relaxing was unlocking their anxiety.

Tracking Tension Release

It's important to become familiar with how your body and nervous system feel when they experience a moment of relief from the constant tension that accompanies anxiety. Even though we have these moments, they are easily swept away by the current of anxiety.

You can use your body to help your nervous system experience and develop a sustainable memory of tension release. After suffering from anxiety for a long time, many people have to relearn what it feels like to be relaxed.

Each day, for one week, take a few moments immediately after swinging your arms or using any of the tensing and relaxing exercises in this part. Use the following chart to note how you feel in each of these nine areas of your body: shoulders, neck, mouth, eyes, elbows, wrists, fingers, shoulder blades, and lower back.

You do not have to be making any particular kind of progress each day. Just take a moment to feel each of these areas of your body after you have completed the exercise. Stand still, see how you feel in each area, and jot down a word or two that expresses the feeling.

Some people wonder why I don't ask them to keep track of how they feel before doing these exercises and then make a comparison afterward. There's a good reason for this. Anxiety makes us tense up, and when we are tense, our ability to feel what is happening in our bodies is blocked. So it is very difficult to actually feel how tense we are. But after a little tension release, our natural sensitivity begins to be restored. *That's* what we need to remember and reacquaint ourselves with.

	Day 1	Day 2	Day 3	Day 4	Day 5	Day 6	Day 7
Shoulders							
Neck							
Mouth							
Eyes							
Elbows							
Wrists							
Fingers							
Shoulder blades							
Lower back							

Standing and Opening

This posture is the next stage in your qigong training. There is a subtle difference between this position and "Starting Wu Ji." If you follow the instructions carefully, you will start to notice the different effect it has on your internal energy and any feelings of anxiety you may have.

Begin by standing in wu ji. Your feet are shoulder-width apart, with your knees gently unlocked, and your feet pointing straight forward. Your arms are loosely by your sides, with your hands gently opened.

Keeping your shoulders and chest completely relaxed, slowly open your elbows out to the sides. The movement is gentle. You feel as if you are softly curving your arms away from your body.

As you stand in this position, you feel a space opening up between your chest and your upper arms. There is more space under your arms. Imagining a small balloon under each arm that supports the weight of your upper arm will help you relax the muscles in your chest, shoulders, and upper arms. Breathe naturally through your nose.

Try remaining in this position, without moving, for a minute or two. Try not to move, allowing your internal energy to find its way throughout your body as it rests in stillness.

Calming the Mind and Body

Now we can go deeper with the practice of wu ji, which you were introduced to in part 1. This practice of "Standing Like a Tree" works on your mind in two ways: by calming the mind and strengthening it. But to strengthen the mind, you first have to calm the mind. Therefore, your training begins with calming the mind.

This process is helpful for working with anxiety, because a calm mind is less likely to panic than an agitated one. In addition, the qigong exercises in this book will help you develop your mental power to the point that you can encourage your body to relax precisely at the moment that you are experiencing high levels of stress.

The inner process of calming the mind begins, in the qigong tradition, with the body. We learn to use the nerves to send signals to our central nervous system. There are nerve endings almost everywhere in our bodies—in our organs, our muscles, and our skin. If we have a physical shock, like an accident, those nerves send emergency signals to our central nervous system, which swings into action. Often it responds with the famous fight-or-flight reaction. This is a good example of how our bodies, through their network of nerves, affect our central command systems. We all feel the impact of strong emotions and thoughts on our cardiovascular system, muscles, and internal organs. This interactive energetic system is what makes qigong work—why we can use the body to calm the mind.

The very first instructions you received on standing still in part 1 included "Calming Your Nervous System," a progressive relaxation technique that starts from the eyes and moves carefully down through the body so that your musculature slowly releases the tension it normally carries all day and night (even during sleep).

After relaxing your face, you carry on an internal conversation with yourself. You invite your muscles to relax, group by group: *I want to relax in the area of my neck.* You tune in to the physical sensations, looking for tension, then feeling the muscle fibers relax. Sometimes you might get distracted, in which case you talk yourself silently through the process: *Now I am relaxing my neck....I am feeling it relax....Now it is relaxing more....I can move on.* You can support the relaxation of your upper body by continuing the process down through your hips, your thighs, your knees, your ankles, the soles of your feet, and your toes.

Once you have completed a full downward sequence of relaxation, start again, beginning again with your eyes. Notice if you have tensed up in the interval. Use that awareness of tension to guide yourself in your relaxation practice. You can do this over and over again while you are standing.

I have noticed that this aspect of inner relaxation while practicing qigong is often overlooked—perhaps because it is invisible. This is the deep inner work that the great masters who practiced this art were able to accomplish. They were not training themselves in physical endurance. They were transforming themselves through profound energy work.

Resting While Standing Still

Despite all your efforts to relax while standing still, you may feel you are becoming tired and tense. One way of relieving this is to reposition your hands so that the backs of your wrists rest in the small of your back, just above your hip bones. Stand like this for a few moments, letting your shoulders completely relax and your wrists sink into the soft flesh in the small of your back.

This is an excellent way of relieving tension in your arms and shoulders while still benefiting from the standing position and allowing a smooth and unobstructed flow of energy through your body. It is an excellent position to use any time you feel anxious, tense, or tired.

Standing deepens our connection with the ever-present energy of the earth. Whether we are in a garden or on the top floor of an office building, we are still able to connect with the potent energy of the earth—the pull of gravity and the earth's magnetism. This energy is always available to us, naturally influencing our state of mind, our emotions, and our inner stability.

Learning to Stay Relaxed

As you work with tension release, using the sensitivity of the body as your guide, you are also increasing your mind's ability to focus on relaxation, experience it, and appreciate it. In this way, although you are exerting yourself mentally and physically, your mind is learning to be active but less agitated. This is not something everyone learns quickly. If you are having trouble relaxing, here are some additional methods used in qigong practice that you may find helpful.

While you are standing, you almost always have thoughts, images, and feelings passing through your mind. You hear and see the world around you. You may become even more aware of your mental activity. You may have some anxiety. Try making a mental note of what you are experiencing: *Now I am feeling anxious. Now I'm worrying about going to the bank.* You don't need to stop thinking and feeling in order to calm down and get over your anxiety. The mind is naturally active. Let these experiences run their natural course. If you feel that your qigong is having no effect at all, you can say to yourself, *This is a very anxious person standing still and continuing to feel anxious.* And continue to stand still. If you experience a lot of anxiety while standing, try listening to a soothing piece of music while you follow the progressive relaxation sequence down through your body.

Inner Powers

In the classical Chinese tradition, a simple smile is said to have a beautiful effect on your whole nervous system. It is said to release a nectar-like substance that bathes all your internal organs.

Try this for yourself. Once you are standing like a tree, bring your attention to your face. Let a gentle smile form. Feel the effect on your eyes, cheeks, and lips. Try using your natural sensitivity to see if you can feel any internal effect on your musculature and organs as you smile gently.

At an international gathering of my students, Madame Wang Yuk Fong, the daughter of Grand Master Wang Xiang Zhai, told them to smile while holding the zhan zhuang qigong postures. "This is the 'inner laughter,'" she said. "That inner happiness will continue through your whole life. The more you stand, the more comfortable you feel. Everything looks very soft, relaxed, and at ease. Yet there is immense power inside you, which—channeled by the mind—expresses itself in movement and power."

"I Never Shook So Much in My Life"

One of my students travels a great deal. One of his trips took him to the Far East, where he was invited to demonstrate the art of tai chi, which he studies with me. It would be part of a large charity event to raise funds for the victims of recent floods. He asked my permission, because he would be demonstrating the form that bears my name—Lam Style Tai Chi. I was happy to support the flood victims and said he could go ahead, but I warned him, "There will be about eight thousand people watching you."

When he returned, he told me that the arena had been completely packed. Luckily, as an international guest, he had a VIP seat at the front and was thrilled to see many masters demonstrating their arts. After a couple of hours, the organizers told him that his turn was coming up, and he went to the locker room to change.

"Then something happened to me that I never experienced before in my life," he told me. "I was completely overcome with intense anxiety and nervousness. I was all alone in that changing room, trembling. I never shook so much in my life. At that point, it was going to be totally impossible for me even to walk out into the arena, let alone demonstrate."

He said, "Then, in the midst of that panic, I remembered the qigong you taught me, but I was so anxious, I couldn't remember anything other than the starting position. I placed my feet shoulder-width apart and stood still, holding the golden ball. I just stood there, shaking, until I noticed that something had begun to change. The extreme shaking started to ease off. My breathing was less shallow; it slowed down a bit. The panic was passing. I was tired, but my mind was clearing."

"So, then what did you do?" I asked him.

He replied, "I heard the announcer call my name. I walked slowly into the arena and did the Lam Style form."

"How did it go?" I asked him.

"I did my best for you," he said, humbly.

Your Standing Experience

You have now been introduced to the qigong practice of "Standing and Opening." This takes you to a deeper level of wu ji, with fresh suggestions on how to calm your mind and body while doing this. As you probably discovered from standing still like this even for a couple of minutes, the body and mind have many sensations. In this age of constant movement, agitation, and distraction, we are not accustomed to simply standing still. Your experience of doing this is important, and I encourage you to take note of what goes on inside you—your physical sensations and all your many thoughts and emotions. Most people experience resistance and discomfort at first, because this is so new. Please keep track of that too. It is a very important part of the overall process of cultivating your internal energy, strength, and resilience. You can use the following chart for your personal notes.

	If you have tried this exercise, what was your initial experience of doing it?	If you have continued to work with this exercise, what effects are you noticing?
"Standing and Opening"		
"Calming the Mind and Body"		
"Resting While Standing Still"		
"Learning to Stay Relaxed"		

"Much More Freedom"

One of my students is a music teacher and a professional pianist. She has been studying music most of her life and gives public performances quite frequently. In addition to being a student of qigong, she is also adept in the Alexander Technique of postural training and teaches that system. What she told me is of value to everyone who suffers from anxiety—not just pianists or other performers.

It takes a lot of energy to teach or perform in public. I have several students who do this and professionals who have come to me for treatment. Part of the challenge they face is that students, audiences, and crowds tend to draw on the energetic strength of the teacher or performer. Being the focus of other people's attention simply sucks out one's own energy. In addition to that, there is the anxiety or nervousness that people naturally feel when having to perform in front of others.

"My breathing used to be much more tense," my student, the pianist, told me. "Practicing qigong has had an enormously beneficial effect. I have noticed that my breathing is much freer when playing. I am therefore less anxious and less dependent on adrenaline and muscle tension when performing in front of an audience."

She said, "The practice of qigong is very grounding. Pianists often practice for long hours with shoulder, neck, and back tension. Learning to hold qigong postures opens energy pathways and reduces muscle tension. As a performer, I've experienced much more freedom in mind and body. I was a very nervous and tense performer in my early career. I now feel much lighter (and even cheerful!) when performing. Being calmer and more centered as a result of doing this work also means that I experience a different sense of time and space."

When I asked her about the relationship of anxiety to her ability to perform, she said, "It's clear. Ask any performer. Anxiety often stops us from responding in the moment and playing with a sense of ease and flow. As a performer, I can say that qigong is invaluable. Standing and sitting in the different energy postures would be a boon to any instrumentalist."

Frequently Asked Questions

What do I do if I feel anxious while doing these exercises?

If you are prone to anxiety, then you know from personal experience that you can feel anxious at any moment, under almost any conditions, and that often it may not even be clear what you are anxious about. Qigong will help you work with the energy of your anxiety and make you much more capable of holding all such experiences in a far stronger field of personal energy.

There are three things you can do if, while doing any of these exercises, you feel anxious:

- Continue with the exercise, whether it is one of the stationary postures or one of the movements. Simply allow yourself to be anxious while doing the practice. This is deep training for your nervous system.

- Stop what you are doing and try the exercise "Working with a Wall," gently bouncing with your upper back off a wall while exhaling. Do this three, six, or nine times, depending on how you are feeling. Most people find that the effect of this practice is to clear their mind and break the grip that powerful emotions can have on our being. It is a nonviolent way of "bringing you around."

- Experiment with an instruction that Grand Master Wang Xiang Zhai gave to his students. He told them to imagine that they were like a great ocean or a great fire. A great ocean has an extraordinary power to absorb and purify. A great fire burns up whatever comes in contact with it. Let your anxiety or any other personal discomfort simply be absorbed and purified in the ocean of your being, or let it enter the healing fire of your energy.

Is there a risk that I could feel even more anxious while standing still?

This can happen, but it is not likely that your anxiety is actually increasing. You are simply noticing it more clearly. It is a little like what happens when you clean your home: you notice all kinds of things that were there all along. If you have this experience, then I recommend you follow the advice I have given in answer to the first question above.

Can I overdo these tension release exercises?

Some people's anxiety can lead them to overdo things. It is hard to overdo these tension and release exercises, because there is a natural wisdom in the body. You get tired and your muscles hurt if you overexert yourself. In my experience, you can trust this automatic safety valve in the body.

Running Out of Anxiety

The energy of anxiety naturally exhausts itself. This is referred to, in poetic fashion, in the *Tao Te Ching*.

High winds do not last all morning.
Heavy rain does not last all day.

It doesn't always feel like it's going to happen, but there comes a point when the intensity of any strong emotion diminishes. The tensing and relaxing exercises I show you in this part of the book naturally support that process of lessening your anxiety. This means, in my experience, that it is almost impossible to hurt yourself doing these exercises. In fact, what happens is that your muscles tire and you naturally stop. But something else happens internally. Your nervous system is automatically involved in the physical alternation between tension and relaxation. Energetically, you could say that the muscular work acts like a suction pump. It draws the energetic whirlpool of your anxiety into the rhythm of tensing and relaxing, which helps to dissipate it.

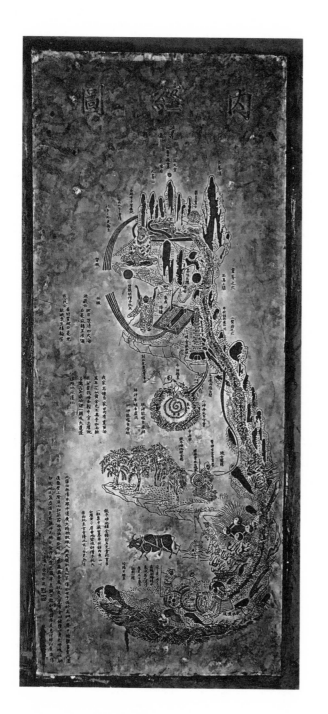

The White Cloud Carving

This mysterious rock carving is often called the "Chart of the Inner Landscape" (the *Neijing tu*). It stands on the grounds of the White Cloud Taoist Temple in Beijing. It is said to be based on a scroll found on Songshan, one of the five sacred mountains of China.

The carving shows a side view of the human body. The head is shown as nine mountain peaks. The eyes are the sun and the moon. The spinal cord takes the form of a powerful river. You can see a sacred pagoda in the region of the throat and lungs. There are bright stars in the area of the heart, a grove of trees in the belly, and a burning cauldron in the lower abdomen.

It is a complete way of understanding the fundamental structures and processes of a human being.

PART 3

Developing Your Inner Strength

Human Energy Patterns

The evocative images of the White Cloud Carving may seem fanciful. They appear to bear no relationship to charts of the human body that are familiar to most of us today. Even if the imaginative drawings were to correspond to the various organs of the body, there seems to be a relationship between them in this model that is different from what we imagine when we think of ourselves as modern people. It is striking that there are multiple sources of powerful activity, and it is not completely clear who is in charge: the mountain sages, the weaver, the oxherd, or the figures tending the cauldron? And what has the greatest influence: the stars, the mountain peaks, the burning fire, the long waterway, or the interplay of yin and yang?

One way of understanding this centuries-old carving—which is a foundational text for practitioners of acupuncture and other systems of Chinese medicine—is to look carefully at how it depicts the human being as an interactive, energetic system, involving many different power spots within an overall complex of forces, profoundly influenced by the natural world and the galaxies.

This tradition of experiencing and working with the total energy of the human being is the basis of the qigong practices in this book. Instead of a separation between mind, spirit, and body, all elements of our being are understood as energetic forces. Their patterns and rhythms exert powerful influences on each other and on our entire being. Thus, properly cultivated, their collective energy can be used for the benefit of the whole person.

It is helpful to understand this—or to accept that it offers an alternative way of understanding the human being—in order to make sense of the value of qigong in dealing with phenomena such as anxiety and fear. Qigong works with patterns of energy in and around the body. Often, like many forms of energy, such as electricity and magnetism, human energy and its movements are invisible. What we experience is its effect.

There are five key aspects of the energetic structure of the human body used in the qigong system. The body is organized around a central column or channel. This runs from the top of the head to the bottom of the torso. Blockages anywhere along this channel seriously disrupt the flow of energy throughout your system. Sitting and standing with your back naturally upright helps prevent or clear such blockages.

At the top of the central channel is the uppermost point of the head. In Chinese medicine, this point is known as *bai hui (ba hui)*, "the hundred meetings." It is sometimes called "the thousand-petaled lotus." This is a particularly sensitive point, through which a person's energy field connects with the energy that surrounds them.

At the other end of the channel is the lowermost point of the torso. This is known as the *huiyin (hui yin)* point, "the meeting of yin." This is a powerful point of connection with the supportive energy of the earth, especially when a person is seated.

In the lower abdomen, just below the navel and a short distance into the body, is the energy reservoir known as the dantien, the "sea of qi." It is the principal area of energy storage within the entire energetic system of the body.

The human being, however, does not exist in isolation. We are at the hub of the energetic forces that surround us at all times. You can imagine that we are standing in the circle of a limitless sphere. It represents the vast and limitless field of energy we call the universe. This circle is not closed or limited. Traditionally, a circle is used in Chinese calligraphy to show open space. It is the symbol of limitless possibilities and all possible configurations of energy, visible and invisible.

Below us is a long curve. It is the uppermost arc of another sphere, one below us—the earth, the vast storehouse of energy that supports all life-forms on our planet and is our traveling home in space.

Since each human being is an energy field, and since energy attracts energy, we act as magnets for the energy that surrounds us. Constant streams of energy come to us and pass through us. The energy from the cosmos tends to be more variable and unstable—it is associated with creativity. The energy from the earth tends to be more constant and stable—it is associated with power. Your qigong practice enables you to harmonize these two forces within your being.

It is within these spheres of energy that we experience life—all that happens to us and the many emotions that are constantly arising like swirling weather patterns. Anxiety is like that. So is fear, thought, and the energy of worrying. Like all energetic patterns, our emotions have great power and great potential. They are part of the total energy system that we learn to work with as our qigong deepens. That's what we'll be working on in this part of the book.

Earth

This calligraphy is the artistic expression of one of the most profound and defining terms in the whole of Chinese culture—the Tao. Normally, "Tao" is translated as "the Way." In the *Tao Te Ching*, the term "Tao" also denotes "earth," meaning everything that surrounds us. Nothing in our environment or our experience is excluded. The earth is all embracing. It gives rise to everything in life—birth, pain, all that we encounter, death, and renewal. As we say in Chinese, it includes "this way" and "that way."

The central image is of a head on top of a body. Underneath, the long brushstroke depicts a long, simple raft in an ever-flowing stream. To the left is a boatman, plying his craft through the earth's waterways.

Taking Root

Let's take your wu ji practice to a deeper level. You do this by developing your connection with the earth. You can do this whether you are standing directly on the earth in a garden or park or on the floor in your home, even if you are in a high-rise apartment.

Begin by standing in the position "Starting Wu Ji," described in part 1. Please follow the relaxation sequence "Calming Your Nervous System" in part 1.

After standing in this position for a couple of minutes, let your mind rest its attention on the soles of your feet. Imagine that you are like a tree with its roots reaching down into the earth. (It may help if someone reads this page to you as you practice.)

A mighty tree is deeply rooted in the earth. Its foundations are unseen. It draws its power from the soil in which it grows. Rising upward to the heavens, the tree's great mass is still. Countless creatures move across its surface, but the sturdy trunk is calm. It is silent and unmoved, filled with energy.

From its tiniest roots deep in the earth to the buds and blossoms far above, the hidden power of the tree is moving, day and night, and season after season. Feeling wind and rain and stretching toward the light, the veins of its innumerable leaves breathe freely in the energy of space.

You are growing in this stillness. Beneath you is the earth, a sphere of power, fertile and immense. It sustains all living beings. As you sink and soften, inwardly relaxed, the earth's great power gives you energy.

Above you, expanding without limit, is the galaxy in which we live. You are standing in a universe of vast, immeasurable power. As you stand, relaxed and vertical, your brain, your senses, and your vital organs open fully, like blossoms in the light. This is the experience we call "Standing Like a Tree." It is deep training for your whole being—your mind, your heart, your nerves, and your internal organs. Outwardly, you are unmoving. You are growing within.

Like the play of water and light in the leaves, like birds making their nests in the branches, like small animals making their way up and down the trunk, all manner of experiences may come to you as you stand. The tree may sway in storms and strong winds, amid thunder and lightning, but it draws strength from its roots. Let your deep training embrace whatever thoughts and feelings, itches or anxieties arise. Don't move, don't scratch. Just stand like a tree, rooted in the earth.

Finding Your Center

Anxiety and other forms of tension often cause us to be off-center. Over the years, we become accustomed to holding our bodies in slightly crooked or tilted postures. The result is that when we stand still, we may notice that we are not properly aligned.

That is why it is very helpful to check to see if you are standing straight while practicing wu ji or any of the other standing practices in this part of the book. As you practice, your inner gyroscope will adjust to the correct, healthy posture.

You can check your posture yourself in a mirror. You can also ask a friend or partner to look carefully at your posture from all sides. Check that you are evenly balanced on your feet, without leaning to one side. Check that your navel is in line with the central point at the top of your head. If you drew a line from the top of your head straight down to the ground, it would pass through your navel and touch the ground exactly at the middle point between your feet.

Make sure that your weight is spread evenly on your feet—that you are not leaning forward or backward. Relax your knees. You can check to see if they are relaxed by locking them tightly and then letting the muscles naturally unlock.

As you stand, you can imagine that the distribution of weight in your body is like that of a pyramid. Your feet are the base. Your head is the peak. The base, spread firmly on the earth, is wide, dark, and heavy. The peak, pointing toward the sky, is upright and light. The feeling of heaviness in your feet comes from connecting with the earth's energy. The lighter sensation in your head is your own awareness of contact with the energy of space.

As you realign yourself in this way, the energetic and structural readjustment of your body has a corresponding effect on your nervous system. The emotional patterns that have been locked into long-standing physical distortions—or have caused the temporary stiffness and tension of a particular day—are freed up as your energy moves without obstruction.

My grand master, Wang Xiang Zhai, told his students, "Begin by standing still. This is the practice that refines the flow of energy throughout the human body. Zhan zhuang transforms the weak into the strong and makes the awkward agile. Stand without moving—each cell will work and grow. Your blood will move at full capacity and bring your vital functions into harmony. You stand in stillness, apparently inert. Within your being, you are filled with strength."

Using the Rolling Pin

If you do a lot of work with a computer, you may have an antistatic mat under your feet at your desk. This is a mat that is normally connected to a grounding wire or an electrical socket to absorb static electricity, which might otherwise damage electronic components. These mats are also helpful in keeping you—the computer user—grounded, as static electricity flows through you down into the mat and is dispersed.

This is a contemporary application of an age-old principle, one that has always been part of the qigong tradition. We are creatures of the earth—we need its energy, and we also need its protection.

Earth energy and our connection with the earth also help dissipate the agitated and erratic emotional energy that we experience as worries, anxieties, and annoyances. In everyday conversation, we call this "settling down."

The earth nurtures and supports all the life-forms we know. The earth's energy bursts forth in spring. It blossoms fully in summer. It yields a rich harvest in autumn. In winter, it regenerates. This energy is always available to us, naturally influencing our state of mind, our emotions, and our inner stability.

Whether we are standing in a garden or on the top floor of an office building, we are still able to connect with the potent energy of the earth. We are always affected by the energetic pull of gravity and the earth's magnetism.

Our standing practice automatically strengthens our connection with the earth.

If you are familiar with acupuncture or reflexology, you know that there is an extremely potent and sensitive point, just behind the ball of the foot, on the central axis of the foot. In Chinese, this is known as the *yongquan* point, the "bubbling spring." It is our principal energetic connection point to the earth. Massaging or pressing this point draws agitated energy in our nervous system downward and helps dissipate it.

One way you can do this is to place a rolling pin, or a pen, pencil, paintbrush, or chopstick under your foot. Roll it backward and forward for a few minutes under the ball and middle of your sole. You can do this sitting or standing. It is not only a refreshing massage. It grounds you, and you'll see the effect on your nervous system.

Holding the Golden Ball at Your Belly

Working with the golden ball in this posture takes your practice of qigong to a more advanced level. It helps your spine decompress, which is beneficial to your central nervous system. The posture also stimulates the circulation of blood and qi throughout the body. Both factors aid our resilience when we are affected by difficult situations, anxiety, and fear.

Begin by standing in wu ji. Your feet should be shoulder-width apart, with your toes pointing forward.

Lower your bottom slightly, about one inch—as if you were about to begin sitting down on a high stool behind you.

Your knees will bend slightly, but do not let them come forward over your toes. You will feel your lower back relaxing, as if you were actually sitting on the high stool. Relax your belly.

Let your hands gently rise up in front of your hips and position them as if you were holding a large golden ball in front of your belly. As you do this, relax your palms. They are gently curved, as if resting on the round surface of the golden ball.

Breathe naturally. To begin with, try remaining in this relaxed position for two minutes.

Easing Your Way Through Tension

Many people experience a lot of tension in the very center of their body. The constant anxiety, worry, and nervous pressure they feel causes them to be stiff in their lower back, hips, intestines, and pelvis. This anxious stiffness cuts off the flow of energy, splitting the body into two. The symptoms are lower backache; hip pain; digestive disorders, including constipation; and groin problems. You could say this is one of the bodily imprints of our anxiety.

By relaxing in this position, holding the golden ball in front of your belly, you may find that these problems ease. As this part of the body relaxes, it has a corresponding effect on the invisible patterns of nervousness, anxiety, and fear.

When holding the golden ball in front of the belly, many people hunch their shoulders and strain their chest muscles. One way to eliminate this unnecessary tension is to imagine that there is a strap running around behind your neck and stretching down to your wrists. The strap takes all the weight of your arms and, at the same time, has the effect of lowering your shoulders and relaxing your chest.

Some people like to do this exercise while actually holding a beach ball or balloon, just to get a clear idea of what it feels like and to get the position correct. This is perfectly fine if it helps you.

It is good to feel that there is something expansive and spacious about the position—so please don't hold the ball too close to you.

It also helps to imagine that you have just had a cup of your favorite warm drink, and its warmth is spreading through your abdomen. You could also imagine the relaxing feeling of a back massage or of a heating pad warming your belly or your lower back. This is the sensation that naturally develops when you hold the golden ball in front of your belly. It is the way your inner energy naturally begins to flow when you allow yourself to relax even for a couple of moments.

Expanding the Golden Ball

If you practice holding the golden ball at your belly for some time, you may feel that it is starting to expand. Sometimes your hands naturally begin to open wider. This is a natural effect of the increased flow of energy.

These sensations point you in the direction of the next practice with the golden ball. You can advance to this next position after you feel you are thoroughly familiar with holding the golden ball at your belly and can do it in a relaxed way for several minutes.

Slowly let your hands open in front of you as if the golden ball was growing wider and wider.

Your elbows remain slightly bent, just as they were when you were holding the ball in front of your belly.

Your palms remain gently curved around the surface of the ball. Your fingers remain gently spread apart.

Your hands should remain the same distance in front of your body as they were when you were holding the ball in front of your belly. They are just moving apart sideways, and they continue to move apart until your fingertips are pointing toward the earth—as you can see in this photo.

Your shoulders are relaxed, and your chest is relaxed. You continue to rest your backside on a high stool, just as you were before. Breathe naturally.

As you stand in this position, the golden ball no longer feels like something you are holding. You feel that in this expansive position, you yourself *are* the golden ball.

"Three Teacups"

In the classical culture of China—and much of the East—there is a story about three teacups. It may help you as you explore the unfamiliar practices in this book and wonder, *Is this actually helping with my anxiety?*

The story goes like this. A master is teaching his students. During a break, he arranges for them all to drink tea together. At a certain point, he places three teacups in a row. One is upside down. One is half full of tea. One is empty. He picks up the teapot and pours out the tea in three equal amounts. The tea spills all over the upside-down cup and runs over the table. The second cup, being already half full, can only hold a little more tea, and soon tea is spilling over onto the table. The third cup is empty. The master is able to fill it completely.

This is not a story about how much information a student can take in. It is about the state of mind of a student who wishes to learn from a master. The master is not simply adding data to the student's mind; the master is transforming the student's being.

The first cup symbolizes the student who is resistant to change. The second cup represents the skeptical student, who takes only from the master what he or she chooses, based what he or she already knows—possibly from another teacher.

The third cup, empty of tea, depicts the being of the student who is completely willing to follow the master's instructions, not out of blind stupidity, but because he or she is open to profound change—and thus to transformative learning.

This attitude of the empty cup does not mean that you should suspend your critical judgment. That is why there are so many charts in this book to help you keep track of your direct, personal experience. But it does mean that second-guessing yourself or the instructions can get in the way of simply doing the practice.

Some students have a long-standing habit of mind, and they might be deeply reluctant to let go of it. Their brains might resist the possibility of change, no matter how much they want to be free of their old patterns. In their case, emptying the teacup just long enough to follow the teacher's instructions could be the first step to that freedom.

Golden Ball Energy Stance

Once you are comfortable holding the golden ball at your belly for several minutes, you can experiment with this more advanced posture. It involves a slightly different stance and a different distribution of your weight. This posture is marvelous for increasing the flow of energy generated by the golden ball practice.

Begin holding the golden ball at your belly with your weight evenly distributed over both your feet.

Shift your weight to your left foot and place your right foot slightly forward and to the right. Point it slightly away from you, toward the right.

Now adjust your weight so that you feel that 60 percent of your weight is on your left foot and 40 percent is on your right foot.

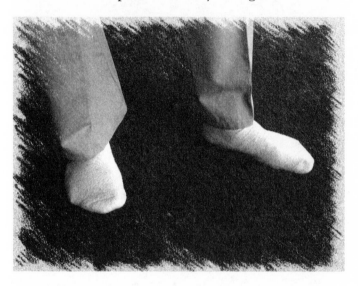

Your knees are relaxed, but not bent. Breathe naturally and stand still in this position for a minute.

Then return to your original position with your feet shoulder-width apart and with your weight spread evenly over both feet. Relax in this position for a moment, still holding the golden ball at your belly. If you find it difficult to continue holding the ball, you can slowly lower your arms to hang loosely by your sides.

Then, move back into the Golden Ball Energy Stance, but this time with your left foot a little forward and pointing slightly toward the left. Place 60 percent of your weight on your right foot, 40 percent on your left. Breathe naturally, and stand still in this position for a minute.

Your arms are still holding the golden ball in a relaxed way in front of your belly. Your palms are gently curved around the surface of the golden ball, with your fingers slightly spread apart.

Although you have changed the position of your feet and shifted your weight, you are still facing forward. Your head is upright. You are still standing straight, holding the golden ball at your belly, but just with more of your weight being borne by your rear leg and foot.

Advancing in This Practice

This stance increases the flow of energy throughout your body. It also strengthens your legs and deepens your connection with earth energy. Once you are able to hold this position for several minutes, you can take the practice to a more advanced level.

The first level is simply holding the position for a longer time. See if you can increase the period of standing to five minutes on each side, separated by an interval of two minutes in which you stand with your weight evenly distributed.

Once you have reached that level, try changing the distribution of your weight so that 70 percent of it is on your rear foot and 30 percent on your front foot. This is more demanding, but it takes you to a higher level of practice. You will likely need to start with shorter periods of time on each side. Then gradually increase to five minutes on each side, separated by an interval of two minutes with your weight evenly distributed.

Deepening Your Experience

In this part of the book, you are being introduced to the deepening practices of connecting with earth energy, taking root, and holding the golden ball at your belly. These are part of the methods used in the qigong tradition to simultaneously develop a person's energy field and produce a state of deep inner relaxation.

Please use the following chart to keep track of your experience. How you respond to these practices will be unique to you. We all have different emotional, physical, and mental responses. The effects can be different on different days and at different times of day. If you find these notes helpful, you can continue to keep notes for yourself on a separate notepad.

	What was your initial experience of doing these exercises?	If you have continued to work with these exercises, what effects are you noticing?
"Taking Root"		
"Using the Rolling Pin"		
"Holding the Golden Ball at Your Belly"		
"Expanding the Golden Ball"		
"Golden Ball Energy Stance"		

Wake Up

The first of the ideograms in this calligraphy means "suddenly," and the second, "understand." We might translate it as "Suddenly, I understand!" or "Wake-up call!"

These brushstrokes express a critical moment, one we've all experienced. We might have read a sentence many times. One day, we read it with fresh eyes; we clap our hands and say, "Oh, now I get it!"

We can also understand this as the moment when we "come to our senses," awakening from a dream or an illusion.

We are floundering in the quicksand of anxiety, fear, and despair. We need to be rescued. "Wake up!" is the help that the energy of qigong offers us.

"I Learned This from My Father"

One day when I was young I saw that my father was very angry. I didn't know what had upset him. Suddenly, there was a startling *crack* as he clapped his hands together very powerfully. I was shocked and immediately cried out, "What are you doing?"

"I'm waking myself up!" he told me, smiling.

"But you are angry and now you are hurting yourself," I protested. I was so worried for him.

"No, my son," he said. "I *was* angry. I could have hurt others. Now everyone is safe; no one has been hurt."

Over the years, I came to understand his words—and what he was doing. It is easy to get swept away on a strong current of thoughts and feelings. We lose ourselves, and we lose track of what's actually happening around us. We are obsessed with something that happened in the past, or we are frantically agitated about something that might happen in the future. We are no longer present. Such moments in which we lose our way can do great harm. They make us forgetful and unaware. We are prone to accidents. We can be flooded with feelings of fear and aggression. Many people who have committed acts of violence speak of being lost to themselves in that moment. That's the mental state my father was waking himself up from. The single clap of his hands discharged it. That's what he meant when he said, "Now everyone is safe; no one has been hurt."

I had a student once who was so angry that he feared he would take out his rage on other people. He was obsessed with computer car games and realized he wanted to kill the imaginary people in the other cars on the screen. He was terrified that his violent obsession would take hold of him when he was driving in traffic. I told him the story of my father, and he understood immediately. Later, he thanked me. He had used this simple method several times. "You saved me—and you saved lives."

This way of waking ourselves up is not the same as self-wounding or being angry with ourselves. This is more like the way some people slap their thighs and shout "I got it!" when they have just solved a difficult problem. It's a way of bringing ourselves back from a daydream—or a waking nightmare of any overwhelming emotion, including anxiety.

Coming Back

When we are overtaken by worry, anxiety, or fear, it can be like being trapped in a nightmare. Sometimes we get lost like that when we are sleeping, and we suddenly wake up in panic. In qigong, getting lost like this is said to result from an imbalance of yin and yang. The soothing effect of qigong practice helps rebalance these energies. If you experience this difficulty at night, please see the sections that follow: "Overwhelmed, Lying Down," "I'm Always Tired and Nervous," and "In the Middle of the Night."

But many people get overwhelmed and end up "lost" during the day. They are awake, but their minds have been captured by a waking nightmare. Our nervous system instinctively knows that we need to wake ourselves up, but on a conscious level, we don't know what to do. The lesson my father taught to me when he clapped demonstrates something you can try.

There are many moments like this, when you intuitively recognize that you need to "come back." Your thoughts might be spinning around and around, trapped in a circle. You might be getting angrier and angrier at someone. Your body might be completely tense with worry—wracked by chest, neck, or back pain.

If you want to break the cycle, clap your hands once, sharply, right in front of you. Notice the effect. It will be different for every person. It is like giving yourself a little energy shock. For a split second, your mind clears.

If you are in an office or another environment where it will be too disturbing to others if you clap your hands, use the back of one hand (your hand can be open or loosely curled—like you are holding an egg) to slap the palm of your other hand, which is quieter. It might hurt for a second or two, but the shock brings you back from your nightmare or paralysis.

You are not punishing yourself or trying to hurt yourself. You are just using your energy to clear your mind for a second and come back into the present moment.

If you don't want to be seen doing this—or if it hurts too much to clap or slap your hands—try using the outside of your thigh. Curl your hand, as if you're holding an egg. Then strike your thigh with the side of your curled hand like you were cracking open the shell of a boiled egg. There is an important meridian (energy pathway) that runs up the outside of the thigh, normally in line with the outside seam of your trousers or jeans. A quick slap or blow on the surface stimulates the energy flow in the meridian, sending a helpful "wake up" jolt to your whole system. You can try this while sitting at your desk. Normally this hardly makes a sound, and no one will see it.

Working with Your Breath

"Take a deep breath," people sometimes say to a friend or coworker who is in a panic, hoping to help him or her calm down. But what do you do if you are in a panic yourself and you want to cool down before things get out of hand?

There are ways you can work with your breathing that can be of long-term benefit—and give you some on-the-spot relief. Feel free to experiment with these. Everyone is unique and responds differently.

Dantien Breathing

Many people breathe by raising and opening their chest cavity. The energy of their breathing is in their upper body. If they are experiencing anxiety and are told to breathe deeply, they will tend to hunch their shoulders and tense their upper body and neck. This has a short-term effect, but it is not as deeply relaxing as it could be.

In the qigong tradition, the focus of our breathing is the dantien in the lower abdomen (see "The Golden Ball" in part 1). It is possible to reorient our breathing using the following simple exercise. It can be done standing, sitting, or lying down. Place your right palm over your abdomen, just below your navel; rest your left palm on the back of your right hand.

As you inhale through your nose, allow your abdomen to expand gently, as if the breath was coming all the way down into it. When you breathe out, let the exhalation start from your abdomen. To begin with, draw your belly in lightly, so that you feel it is gently squeezing the air out of your lungs. If you practice this over time, your breathing will return to the original deep pattern you were born with.

Double Breathing

If you feel the need to boost your energy vitality in the midst of a difficult situation or a fit of anxiety, try this special breathing. Breathe in twice through your nose; that is, make two short, quick inhalations in succession. Then breathe out through your mouth. You feel you are blowing stale air out of your body.

When you inhale twice quickly, you are taking in double the oxygen you normally inhale. And when you exhale, blowing stale air out of your body, you are dispelling a larger volume of carbon dioxide from your lungs than you normally do. In the classical Chinese way of understanding the body, this is described as taking in double the qi and then clearing stale qi from your energy field.

Try this double breathing six times. Don't keep on doing it: it is only for a quick boost. If you then want to continue with another practice, do some of the standing qigong exercises in this book.

Overwhelmed, Lying Down

Many people who suffer from anxiety feel constantly exhausted. The nervous effort of coping with anxiety makes us want to lie down and rest. But often we don't find resting easy—the mind continues to spin, and we end up simply carrying on worrying while lying down. You may find the following gentle qigong practice helpful when you are tired and want to lie down or when you are lying down but still feeling anxious. It both relaxes and energizes you. This is also a wonderful way to start your day.

Lie flat on your back, with your head resting on the floor or the bed. Your arms are to your sides, slightly away from your body, with your hands positioned so that your palms are facing upward. Please sink into this position for a minute.

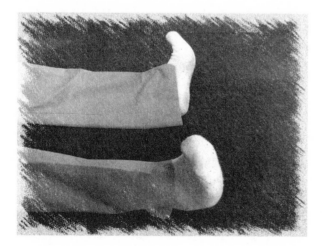

Then, keeping your heels on the floor or bed, stretch your toes up so that your feet are at right angles with your legs. You'll feel a little stretch in the backs of your legs.

Then lift your head slightly off the floor or the bed and look down toward your raised toes. Keep your gaze on your feet while you breathe in and hold your breath for a few seconds. Then breathe out and completely relax. Allow your feet to return to their original, relaxed position, and let your head sink back down to rest on the floor or bed. Repeat this six times—breathing in as you move into the position, out as you relax.

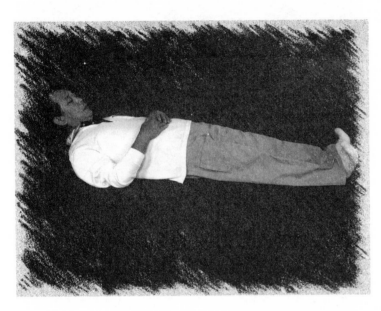

Once you are familiar with this basic movement, you can add a little energy work to further increase the flow of energy throughout your body. Imagine an energy circuit running from the ball of one foot to the other. From the ball of your left foot, let the energy travel up to the top of your head and then back down to the ball of your right foot.

At first, you will need to imagine this energy circuit. Gradually, you will feel it. Try to keep your mind attentive to this energy flow while you are gazing down at your feet, holding your breath. When you breathe out, lower your head, and relax, you may feel the energy continuing to flow, but there is no need to concentrate on it.

Then scan your entire body to see how you are feeling. You may feel like you want to get up. You may want to sleep. If you want to repeat this exercise, please wait a few minutes before repeating it, and you should only do it a total of three times in any one day. If you have enough energy to want to keep doing qigong exercises, then I recommend you get up and do some of the standing practices in this book.

If you have trouble falling asleep, you can use this practice when you get into bed. If you suffer from insomnia, you can try this in the middle of the night. For many people, it has an almost immediate effect. But if you are still having trouble getting back to sleep, there is a more powerful method in the pages that follow, called "In the Middle of the Night."

"I Am Always Tired and Nervous"

One of my students in London is a real estate agent. He told me, "I am always tired and nervous." The nature of his work is mentally strenuous and physically demanding.

Several years ago he woke up in the middle of the night, which was common for him at the time. He was always on edge and couldn't sleep through the night. He turned on the television and saw my show, *Stand Still—Be Fit*. The next week, he came to see me, and he has continued with me ever since.

He still has a lot of pressure in his job. Qigong does not magically get rid of anything that could cause him anxiety. It is really about helping him have good energy that, like a horse carrying a rider, can support him no matter what he is going through. Recently he told me about a nightmare he had had.

I believe this internal energy work helps even my subconscious. I dreamed that I was chased by zombies into a huge barn. The dream was so real; it was frightening. I was screaming and running faster and faster. Suddenly I saw a gap in the top of the wall near the ceiling. I took an enormous, superhuman jump, squeezed through the gap, landed on open ground, and was safe. But my dream continued, and in it the whole town was swept away by a huge tidal wave. People were drowning and screaming. Properties crumpled down. The wind was howling. Trees were blown down. My entire house, except the roof, was submerged under water. Yet I was safe, as I was squatting on top of the roof in a sea of water. I woke up. I was dry. And do you know why? It is because my body energy was strong and warm. At some level, I was aware of this, and even in that nightmare, I could not fall into the water. I believe this is the effect of this practice, deep inside me.

In the Middle of the Night

You may suffer from sleeplessness, either having trouble getting to sleep or waking up in the middle of the night with your mind racing. Some people are completely overtaken by anxieties. They know they need a good night's sleep, but they just can't get it. I have found that many people are helped by this simple exercise that can be done lying in bed or on the floor. It is a variation on the exercise "Overwhelmed, Lying Down."

Lie flat on your back, your arms resting by your sides. Your head is resting on the floor or the bed. Keeping your heels on the floor or bed, pull your toes up so that your feet are at right angles to your legs. You feel the stretch in the backs of your legs.

Then turn your palms toward the sides of your thighs. Clench your fists. Pull your fists in toward your wrists so that they curl toward you, and you feel a strong stretch in your wrists. Squeeze your fists as strongly as you can.

As you do this, lift your head slightly off the floor or the bed and look down toward your toes. Breathe in and hold your breath for a few seconds.

Breathe out and completely relax. Let your feet return to their original, relaxed position, let your hands relax, and let your head sink back down.

Repeat this six times—breathing in as you move into the position, out as you relax.

Waking Up Your Experience

At this point in part 3 you have been experimenting with practices that aim to wake you up or bring you back from daydreams, nightmares, or difficult situations, often involving high levels of anxiety. These including "Coming Back," "Dantien Breathing," "Double Breathing," and practices you can do while lying down or experiencing sleeplessness.

Please use the following chart to keep track of your experience. The effects can vary on different days and at different times of day. If you find this helpful, continue to keep notes for yourself on a separate notepad.

First, please reflect on your overall experience of trying the "wake up" practices below from this part of the book. Have you noticed a general effect on your energy levels when you try these "wake up" practices?

Now, please reflect on your experience of the individual practices listed below.

	What was your initial experience of doing it?	If you have continued to work with this exercise, what effects are you noticing?
"Coming Back"		
"Dantien Breathing"		
"Double Breathing"		
"Overwhelmed, Lying Down"		
"In the Middle of the Night"		

"Their Eyes Become Brighter"

One of my students is a former cardiac and intensive care nurse who now teaches zhan zhuang to senior citizens in London. She is a former senior administrator for Amnesty International.

She told me, "I have reserves of energy and resilience that enable me to carry on even when feeling tired. These exercises have affected me mentally. Learning to stand still has a calming effect; it gives me more self-confidence and has reduced my tendency to be hypercritical, of myself and others. I used to suffer from nonspecific anxiety, which I experience far less now. Qigong has also helped me to understand and tolerate pain."

I asked her about the experience of the senior citizens whom she now teaches.

Many of them are over sixty years of age, and many have some form of disability. Apart from the physical benefits of qigong, they report that the practice has a calming and relaxing effect, and that it helps them to sleep—they sometimes visualize doing these exercises or standing or sitting still while lying in bed. It reduces their underlying anxiety, which they often experience as muscular tension. As they become more familiar with their body, they learn to use only the muscles needed and to let go of the others.

What I see in all my classes is the way, over time, the students' posture improves—they are standing or sitting with a stronger back. But the effect is more than physical. Their eyes become brighter.

So many of them say that qigong has boosted their self-confidence and reduced the level of fear they might feel. One gentleman told me it felt that this had opened up a whole new world to him and had a profound effect on his spiritual life.

Your Daily Routine

If you would like to develop and strengthen your qigong practice, I highly recommend that you experiment with a short daily sequence. How you start your day has a deep influence on your physical, mental, and emotional state throughout the day's events. A short morning routine will help clear your internal energy pathways, so that your energy is naturally able to absorb any anxiety, fear, or other strong feelings you might have during the day.

You could experiment with the following qigong energy-strengthening sequence before you get carried away with the day's worries—even before you reach for your phone or your computer. Of course, you may have many thoughts and worries while you do this, but just let all those thoughts and feelings arise as you do your qigong. The following sequence, drawn from the practices in this book, will take you less than ten minutes a day.

Begin in bed. Lie flat on your back, arms resting beside you. Stretch your toes up and lift your head to look at your toes. ("Overwhelmed, Lying Down," part 3)
Sit up on the edge of your bed. Place your feet flat on the floor. Sit still for about a minute. ("Sitting Up," part 1)
Get up. Use the toilet if you need to. Make yourself a cup of warm water (not tea or coffee, and not too hot) and drink it.
Stand still, preferably where there is some fresh air coming in. Practice arm swinging. One hundred arm swings will take you less than two minutes. You can do more if you wish! ("Arm Swinging," part 2)
Slowly move your arms to your sides so that you are standing in wu ji. Practice the relaxation sequence, starting with your eyes and scanning down through your body to release any overnight tension. Remain in wu ji for two minutes as you do this. ("Starting Wu Ji," part 1)
Remain standing. Slowly move your arms in front of you to hold the golden ball in front of your belly. Relax your shoulders. Hold this position for a minute. ("Holding the Golden Ball at Your Belly," part 3)
Practice twisting, tensing, and then relaxing your hands twelve times. This will take you about a minute. ("Tensing and Relaxing," part 2)
Stand in the "Gathering Your Energy" posture for a minute to close the routine. ("Gathering Your Energy," part 1)

Now you are ready to start your day.

Frequently Asked Questions

What do I do if I can't stand still in wu ji or hold the golden ball long enough?

Please don't overdo any of these practices. You are not in a competition—either with yourself or with others. Please don't strain yourself. At the beginning, you will experience many different sensations. Some people get impatient. Some people get bored. Some people experience aches and pains. Some people feel nothing. This is all part of the way qigong works on your nervous system. Set yourself a clear target for your practice. But if you feel you need to stop sooner, that's fine. You need to pay attention to your own experience and be guided by your own natural wisdom.

Is it normal to shake while doing qigong?

Shaking is perfectly normal. As you hold the positions, your muscles slowly tire. The parts of the muscles that you normally use may reach the limits of their endurance and call on the remaining parts of the muscles to help. This is the point—a stage beyond tension—at which you may begin to tremble. The shaking may then become more vigorous. That's natural. Don't try to stop shaking. You will gradually find yourself shaking less and less. For long periods, you may not shake at all. Relax in the position as much as you can. If you relax as much as you can, you will have taken your body and mind to a new level of development.

Is something wrong if one side of my body feels different than the other?

Nothing at all. As you stand, one leg may feel longer than the other. One finger can be hot; another, cold. In the qigong tradition, these are signs that your internal energy is beginning to rebalance itself. At first you notice imbalances of which you may have been completely unaware. Normally, your body naturally rebalances itself. The initial experience of asymmetry is a sign that your training is working.

Is something wrong if my feet feel odd?

This is natural. Our lives are so busy that we rarely have time to be still. When we sit or stand still for a little while, our nervous systems react. Some people find that their feet feel hot when they first stand in qigong postures. Sometimes they get pins and needles.

These are the natural sensations of your feet bearing the relaxed weight of your body and making a powerful connection to the energy of the earth.

Does qigong affect my digestion?

Qigong improves the flow of energy throughout your entire body, including all your internal organs. Sometimes people are surprised to find their stomachs rumbling or to experience burping and flatulence when they are doing these exercises. This is all part of qigong waking up your system. I recommend that you drink a glass of warm water before doing qigong training, especially if you start a daily routine. Never overeat. Chew your food thoroughly before swallowing. That helps your digestion—whether you are doing qigong or not.

Adding Another String to Your Bow

A lot of people take their anxiety personally. Because it is disturbing and makes them feel so uncomfortable, they tend to think that they might be doing something wrong—they attribute it to a personal weakness or failure. But there is a completely different way of thinking about it. When I talked with my own master about his life experience—he died recently in his mid-nineties—he talked about the power of stillness. He pointed out how little we have of that nowadays and how much the world had sped up around us. If you look at our modern lifestyle, you could say that we live in a culture of anxiety. This is constantly affecting our experiences, our attitudes, and our nervous system.

We are all looking for ways to cope with this constant tide of anxiety. So please don't think that it is somehow your fault that you feel this way. The question is how best to help our nervous systems cope with the circumstances in which we find ourselves. I like to think that learning qigong adds another string to our bow. It gives us one more option in life. If it helps us to calm down and cope better with our own experience of anxiety, then it will also have a positive effect on everyone we come in contact with. They will experience your energy like a light breeze on a hot day.

Senses

These thirteen strokes form the character "yi." This comes close to representing what we mean by the word "senses." "Yi" embraces the dimension of thought, feeling, and emotion in the human person.

The notion of "yi" is central to the Chinese tradition of meditation. According to this tradition's understanding of consciousness, awareness is like a movie screen. It receives the passing imprint of whatever is projected onto it. The screen itself is not changed. It is ready to receive whatever is projected onto it. It remains fresh, like a sheet of white paper on which calligraphy can be drawn.

Fear, anxiety, and all forms of mental disturbance are like these projections on a screen. Whatever we experience through our senses is also displayed on the screen. If we are aware of the evanescent, yet potent, nature of the senses, we can use our senses to tame and vanquish our demons.

PART 4

Using the Power of Your Senses

Using the Power of Your Senses

We can use the power and sensitivity of our senses to reorient and rebalance our nervous system. We can draw on their power to influence our mental activity and any related physical symptoms. We can use them to help us work with even the most deep-seated patterns conditioned by anxiety, fear, and other emotional states.

Some people find this hard to imagine. They are so used to experiencing recurrent and troubling states of mind that they believe these are immutable. "That's just the way I am," people tell me.

There is also a widespread assumption that the body and mind are somehow distinct entities—two different systems. They may be connected and working in parallel, but they are separate. This has long been reflected in some medical systems, with different methodologies of diagnosis and care for the mind and for the body. Since the senses are associated with physical sensation—and thus the body—the notion that they could have a powerful, even integrated, influence on our mental state runs counter to this deep-seated assumption of separateness.

These days, around the world, the study and treatment of the mind and the body are coming ever closer together. A more integrated medical model is emerging. Interestingly, the way we talk about our mental states in casual conversation already points to an intuitive awareness of this unity. We frequently rely on metaphors from our bodies and our senses to describe our elusive emotions: "I'm so angry I can't see straight." "I'm all knotted up with anxiety." "I feel uptight." "I'm under such pressure." "I'm stewing in this." "I feel so raw." "I'm so touched by your love." "Your grief is palpable."

In the qigong tradition, the so-called mind-body split does not need to be healed. It never existed. The human being is understood to be a single, complex field of energy. This is very similar to the latest studies and models developed in the field of quantum physics. It could be said that some energetic patterns are more dense and others are more ethereal, but there is no separation between mind and matter. Therefore, we are a living totality, which is constantly manifesting and influenced by innumerable tendencies—both those that arise within our own field of energy and those that influence us from the immeasurable energetic field of the universe.

Both our senses and our mental states are part of this vibrating field of awareness. A single thought can cause our hearts to skip a beat. A single breath of fresh air can open our minds. This is the fundamental understanding on which the experiments and suggestions in this part of the book are based. They are not theoretical notions or new age fantasies. They are based on centuries of careful study, meticulous attention to detail, and the deep care of the qigong tradition.

The simple suggestions in the following pages may seem lightweight. For example, to suggest that burning a stick of incense could ease the paralysis of fear may seem nonsensical—and might even feel insulting to the person who is caught in the icy grip of terror. But from an energetic point of view, pain and mental suffering is almost inevitably associated with blocked energy—in the same way that ice impedes the flow of a great river. There is often a congealed, stagnant quality to the experience of being distressed, overwhelmed, and in despair. Like anything that is frozen, these mental states respond instinctively to warmth, expansiveness, and a widened horizon of awareness. This is so natural that we don't even need incense. We experience it every time we breathe the fresh air of the countryside, hear the sound of a nearby stream, and see birds taking wing in the sunlight.

Understanding this and being able to use the fundamental energy of our being in this way is a path to human empowerment. It allows us to use all the faculties and energies of our being and to make a healthy relationship with our own energy and the natural energy of the living world around us.

Sight

The Chinese character "ngan" represents "sight" or, more correctly, the process of seeing. The square on the left-hand side contains two dots, representing our eyes. In the classical Chinese tradition, seeing is understood to be a two-way process. It involves the mind's receptivity to light entering the eyes and transmitting its energetic messages to the consciousness. It also involves the radiant power of the mind reaching out beyond itself—through the eyes—to the world around us.

In the qigong tradition, the eye is a gateway for the energy that surrounds us. It is like a telescopic dish receiving the signals of the galaxy.

Looking into a Glass of Water

Whether you are currently experiencing anxiety or are in a situation that might produce anxiety, you can experiment with using your visual sense to affect your nervous system. As with any experiment, you do not have to believe it will work. You can adopt the approach of a scientist, carefully examining your experience to see the results. It is important to remember that in the qigong tradition, your entire being is a field of energy. Therefore, whatever happens to any part of your body or mind has an influence on your entire energy field. It is like adding a drop of watercolor paint to a glass of water—the pigment diffuses throughout the liquid.

In the calligraphy for "senses" that opens this part of the book, you are introduced to the notion that the mind, like a sheet of white calligraphy paper, absorbs and reflects back whatever is painted upon it. Thus, while we may feel that our anxieties or fears operate at a deep level of the mind (whereas our sensory experiences are superficial), our senses are influencing the mind, like the strokes of a brush on paper. Therefore, we can use the power of our sensory experience to draw the mind in any direction, at any moment. Please bear this in mind as you experiment with these practices.

We can use the sight of water in numerous ways to literally keep our stream of thought fluid. The colors blue and green, which are reminiscent of the sea, have a similar effect. These can also be combined. If you have a blue- or green-tinted glass, fill it with water and place it on a table near you, so you can gaze at it comfortably. Rest your attention on the glass of water for a minute or so. Feel free to let any thoughts or feelings arise in your mind and heart. We are not trying to combat or suppress your natural feelings. We are simply letting the water and the blue or green color register in your visual field of consciousness.

The great qigong master Wang Xiang Zhai advised his students to imagine that they themselves were like a vast ocean. The ocean's immense and deep waters are home to inconceivable life-forms. Its waters have unknown depths. It is capable of accepting, absorbing, and purifying whatever enters it. In the following chart, you can record your experience of using a glass of water to imagine yourself this way.

Here is another experiment. In Chinese businesses, you often see decorative fish tanks, which are kept (in homes as well as places of work) because of their impact on the environment. They have a beneficial effect on everyone who spends time there. If you have an aquarium yourself, you can experiment with standing or sitting a short distance from it and gazing at the life taking place within the tank. You may find it especially helpful to pay attention to one fish in particular. Observe it closely, follow its movements, watch the subtle patterns of its breathing and the delicate movements of its fins as it glides or floats in the water. If you wish to deepen this practice, see if you can identify with the fish or imagine what it might be like to be this supple being moving and floating in the waters of the tank. Allow yourself to feel that you yourself are that very fish.

You might be quite skeptical about whether this would have any effect on you, particularly if you are a highly intelligent, rational, and productive person, coping with many demands on you. You might say to yourself, *How on earth will staring at a guppy make a difference when I should have left for the office ten minutes ago?* I can't answer that question for you. I can only suggest that you give it a try.

You can also experiment with the soothing power of candlelight. It is not accidental that people in virtually all cultures enjoy the subtle influence of candlelight. We may associate it with romance, but it is by no means limited to that. If you are working at home, having a meal, spending time with friends or family, or even rushing about frantically, see what happens if you light a candle. You don't have to stop and stare at it. Its light will influence the environment around you, even if you barely have time to notice it. But since this is an experiment, see if you can notice the subtle soothing and warming influence of this silent beacon.

Working with Sight

Use the following chart to record your impressions of the experiments for using the power of sight to influence your state of mind. Often their impact is subtle, but you may notice their influence in your body, your physical movements, your personal habits, the way you speak, and the things you notice in your environment.

	If you have tried using your sight impressions in this way, what was your initial experience of doing it?	If you have continued to work with this approach, what effects are you noticing?
Working with a blue- or green-tinted glass of water.		
Working with the ocean imagery of Grand Master Wang Xiang Zhai.		
Working with an aquarium.		
Working with candlelight.		

Sound

This simple character is "yih." It depicts the human ear. Like the eyes, our ears are a bridge between our nervous system and the world around us.

We tend to think of the ear as an organ of hearing, but it is more than that. Deep within its structure is the delicate mechanism that governs balance. In some medical systems, this balance is thought of as a physical process. But in the tradition of classical Chinese medicine, balance is both inner and outer, spiritual and physical. This book is about both, using the power of the body to influence the workings of the mind. True balance is being able not only to stand upright but also to absorb in one's being the shock of the unexpected and the destabilization of anxiety.

Listening to the Garden

We all know that sounds have a profound influence on our mind and nervous system. Everybody is familiar with the effect of changing the soundtrack behind film footage. If we are shown a group of people running down the street accompanied by tinkling piano music, our minds—without any verbal explanation—jump to the conclusion that this is a happy scene. If we see exactly the same footage accompanied by the slow, sonorous notes of a cello, most of us instantly believe that we are about to watch something dreadful happen. Similarly, if someone screams—even without words—we are likely to be startled and upset. If we walk into a room where soft, flowing music is being played, we are likely to feel our bodies relaxing.

Obviously, we cannot control everything we hear, especially living in an age of constant noise: machines beeping or humming, phones ringing or vibrating, cars honking. But we can influence our sonic field in ways that relax, nurture, and strengthen our nervous system. Sometimes we just have to pay attention to sounds that are all around us—but may not be those we notice most.

When you awaken in the morning, before turning on the radio, checking your smartphone, or jumping out of bed, listen for the sound of the sparrows or other small birds that might be outside your window, twittering in a nearby garden. Particularly if you have had a stressful night, slept fitfully, or are waking up to a stressful day, I recommend the experiment of letting the music of these songbirds, however faint or distant, into the space of your mind.

Listening to water, in its many forms, can also have a potent effect on our nervous system. This is why many people place a small fountain somewhere in their home and increasingly in their offices or work cubicles.

You can also experiment with music. Wherever I teach qigong, I always try to have a recording of soft instrumental music playing. This influences the nervous system of my students, calming their minds and relaxing them so that they are more able to benefit from the power of qigong practice. A very helpful experiment is to listen to different types of music as you practice the qigong exercises in parts 1, 2, and 3 of this book. Notice the influence of different kinds of music. Try to see which music has the deepest and most helpful effect on your practice.

Many people like to listen to their favorite music as they work, an example of the ancient truth about the influence of sound that has made its way into the modern world.

Working with Sound

You can use the following chart to record your impressions of the experiments for using the power of sound to influence your state of mind. The impact of this experiment with your senses is subtle. You may notice its influence in your body, your physical movements, your personal habits, the way you speak, and how you feel about what takes place around you.

	If you have tried experiencing sound in this way, what was your initial experience of doing it?	If you have continued to work with this approach, what effects are you noticing?
Working with the sounds of birds.		
Working with the sound of water.		
Working with music while doing qigong.		
Working with different types of music while doing qigong.		

"The Reset Button of My Mind"

One of my students works for the local governing council of a district in London. For almost as long as I have known her, she has cycled to and from her work and to our qigong classes. Recently she told me about an incident that made a deep impression on her.

I was cycling home from work one day and felt very upset and anxious about a number of problems that I was having at work. In fact, I wasn't paying much attention to the road or the cars as I cycled along. There were many things that I was worrying about. My mind was completely absorbed in my difficulties.

Suddenly, I heard the sound of a bird. Even though I was cycling in traffic, somehow the call of that bird penetrated everything else, and I heard it very, very clearly. It was so startling that I pulled over to the side of the road, got off my bike, and stood on the pavement looking up into the trees to see if I could spot the bird.

I was overcome with the wonder of the world. I must have stood there for quite a few moments, looking up into the trees and listening to the bird's song.

I remember this incident vividly, because when I got back on my bike and carried on cycling home, my mood had completely changed. Before, I was weighed down with my worries, anxieties, and all the things that were going wrong. But when I got back on my bike, I felt so much lighter in my spirit. I didn't even go back to thinking about the problems I was so anxious about.

It's not that those problems weren't serious. They were real difficulties I was having at work. The difference was my attitude or, perhaps you could say, my inner approach. Before, it was as if my mind was being crushed by what I was facing. I was in a tunnel. Afterward, my mind felt refreshed, no longer dragged down. Later on, I had a lot more clarity and some really good ideas about what I could do at work the next day. It was as if hearing the sound of that bird somehow pressed the reset button of my mind.

It wasn't just that she heard the sound of the bird. She paid attention to it, stopped, and listened.

Smell

This noble character is "bei"; it depicts the human nose. This is not easy to see, because the character comprises many different elements—the human person, feeling, two legs, and two hands.

This complexity, almost like a portrait of the entire human being, reflects the incredible way in which smell is capable of affecting our entire being. It is said that of all our senses, smell has the most immediate effect on our brain. A single odor can affect our entire body—a perfume enchants us; a stench makes us shudder.

Knowing this, we can use the power of smell to affect our state of mind, sedate pain, and awaken our sleeping spirit.

Scenting the Sweet Smell

Smells have a very powerful effect on our nervous system. In this day and age, we may think of smells as merely atmospheric background to our experience, but they are constantly at work on us. They can affect our entire central nervous system. They can seduce us. They can jolt us awake. They can heal us. They can cause collapse. In traditional Chinese medicine, if a person was severely ill and too weak to eat, he or she would be subjected to strong, putrid odors—so repulsive that the person would vomit. The effect was to jump-start the digestive system. It was an extreme measure, but it could save a life. Thus, even a terrible smell can be used to good effect on our mental and physical state. But don't worry, I'm not going to suggest that you try that!

There are some simple and obvious things you can experiment with. In the Far East—and increasingly in the West—many people use incense to create a warm and inviting feeling in their homes. Many people associate incense with religious ritual, but it can be used in a completely secular way. If you are free from smoke allergies, try burning some sandalwood or another incense in the room where you work or at home or when you are spending time with friends or family. There is now a wide range of fragrances available. You can experiment with different scents.

If you don't like incense, try aromatic oils—there is a wonderful variety now available. Or you can try an aromatic candle. These are used to dispel stale and offensive odors in the home, but they can also be used simply to diffuse a gentle scent throughout the environment. If you have trouble sleeping, try the well-known method of using a lavender sachet or eye pillows filled with lavender.

As the calligraphy for "smell" suggests, the power of our olfactory system is so strong that it affects our entire central nervous system, more than any other of our senses. So while your anxiety or fear may seem overwhelming, impenetrable, or unshakeable, it is not necessarily immune to the subtle, healing influence of a sweet smell.

Working with Smell

You can use the following chart to record your impressions of using the power of smell to influence your state of mind. Often, the impact of these experiments is very subtle, but you may notice their impact in your body, your physical movements, your personal habits, the way you speak, and how you experience things around you. Remember that even an unpleasant experience can shift your state of mind.

	If you have tried using your sense of smell in this way, what was your initial experience of doing it?	If you have continued to work with this approach, what effects are you noticing?
Working with incense.		
Working with aromatic oils or fragrant candles.		
Working with lavender.		

Taste

If you look carefully at the brushstrokes of this character, "tsih," you will see at the bottom an open mouth. Above it is a long horizontal line, which represents the outstretched arms of a human being. It is like a child spreading his or her hands on a table and reaching forward to grasp a bowl of soup.

Every taste has a subtle—and sometimes not so subtle—effect on the inner core of our being. Indeed, the mouth plays an extremely important role in the Chinese medical diagnostic system. There are three main methods of diagnosis: taking the pulse, examining the eyes, and studying the tongue. Meticulous observation of the tongue is said to be the closest we can get—without invasive procedures—to observing the internal organs of the body. A skilled practitioner can read not only the state of the body but also our emotions in the subtle patterns of our tongue.

Taking a Cup of Tea

In Chinese culture, we say you never forget the food you had at home as a child. The texture, aroma, and taste of that food remains imprinted in our memories for the rest of our lives. It is not only true of our childhood. Taste has a lingering effect on us. Our memories of important moments of our lives often include a recollection of something we tasted at that time.

In this modern era, when so many people experience stress and persistent anxiety in their lives, it is not surprising that we also witness an increase in the consumption of "junk food." We seek comfort and emotional release in the tantalizing flavors that are carefully blended in these foods, even though they have low nutritional value. The fact that junk food is of poor quality should not distract us from an age-old truth—the taste of something sweet calms the spirit. For example, in Chinese cuisine, we prepare sweet rice, sometimes known as "sticky rice." It has both a savory and a sweet taste and is normally served wrapped in a lotus leaf. In traditional Chinese medicine, sweet flavors are beneficial to the spleen and the earth energy of the body. A delicious taste is said to make the mouth calm and happy. The sensation is received by the brain and transmitted to the central nervous system. Similarly, if we want to wake up, there is nothing like chili powder or a curry. Our energy surges just from the aroma, even before we experience the taste.

So what should you do if you want to use the power of taste in an intelligent way and not succumb to the unhealthy eating habits of the modern world? There is an ancient tradition—famous in China, but also enjoyed throughout the rest of the world—that I highly recommend: drinking tea. Drinking a cup of tea is a way of engaging all our senses in a sophisticated way. There's the shimmering surface of the tea in the cup, the aroma that arises from the steaming tea, the delightful sound of the tea being poured from the pot into the cup, the warmth of the cup in your hands, and the taste of the tea itself. Every culture has its own version of a tea ceremony. Whether it is in a Middle Eastern market, a stately home in Europe, a Japanese teahouse, an Indian garden, or a Western restaurant, tea works its magic.

In many parts of the world, a good cup of coffee—carefully brewed from fine-quality beans—has taken the place of tea. What's important to remember, whether your choice of beverage is tea, coffee, or anything else, is that there is more to this than sipping or gulping down a drink. It's a gathering together of many, many elements of the lives we lead together, the richness of the natural world, and our appreciation of being alive.

The next time anxiety gets the better of you, I suggest a moment of world culture—the age-old cup of tea, a good cup of coffee, or whatever you would love to taste.

Working with Taste

You can use the following chart to record your impressions of the suggestions and experiments for using the power of taste to influence your state of mind. Often the impact of these experiments is very subtle, but you may notice their impact in your body, your personal habits, the way you speak, and how you relate to other people.

	If you have tried using your taste sense in this way, what was your initial experience of doing it?	If you have continued to work with this approach, what effects are you noticing?
Working with sweet flavors.		
Working with spices and savory flavors.		
Working with tea, coffee, or another beverage.		

Touch

You may recognize this character. We saw it in the calligraphy for "human being." It means "body" and can be understood as "touch." From the topknot at the uppermost tip of this ideogram through the ends of the brushstrokes that depict the legs and feet, it tells us that the entire human body is exquisitely sensitive.

It is not only the physical body that is capable of feeling. We are blessed with a nervous system that reaches throughout our entire physical structure and is endlessly responsive to the most delicate of influences.

Sometimes, especially when we are anxious, distressed, or fearful, this sensitivity can be mistaken for weakness; but it can also be one of our greatest strengths. It all depends on how we use it.

Feeling What Touches Us

The calligraphy for "touch" shows the whole body from head to toe. This was the classical, poetic way of expressing the tactile receptivity of our bodies. Oddly enough, we often underestimate the power of touch, yet we are constantly experiencing it across the entire surface of our skin.

We feel the air and the atmosphere around us on our head, hands, and other exposed parts of our bodies. We feel our clothes brushing against us, from the shoes or sandals on our feet to the collars of our shirts. We feel the objects we hold in our hands and often greet each other with a handshake, a gentle touch, or a hug. When we cry, we feel the tears on our cheeks and cover our eyes with our hands. We embrace someone we love. When we shower, we feel water cascading over our faces and bodies. A massage rejuvenates and relaxes us. This entire nonverbal field of experience is constantly sending messages to our nervous system, affecting our emotions and shaping our experience of life.

If you are anxious or overwhelmed by the pace of life, there are three ways in which the power of touch may help you find a greater sense of equilibrium, nurture, and inner delight. The first is to ask yourself how you feel. Normally, we think only of our mental and emotional state: "I feel upset," "I feel overwhelmed," "I feel afraid." But while you are experiencing those emotions, your entire body is also sensing the environment around you, feeling the clothes you are wearing, the phone in your hand, the cup from which you are drinking. Try taking a moment to extend your consciousness to this entire field of sensation and notice the effect.

Pay attention to the clothes you are wearing. Do they feel delightful and comforting to your skin? They don't have to be expensive or elegant. Next time you choose something to wear, don't consider only how it looks. Ask yourself how it feels, because you may be spending the rest of your day in contact with it.

Whenever we experience a sudden shock, like losing our balance or getting bad news, we instinctively reach for something to hold. We can use this innate body wisdom to help us. It's not accidental or a sign of human weakness that progressive clinics and health-care centers often have soft toys on the chairs and sofas of their waiting rooms. An adult holding a teddy bear does not indicate infantile regression. We all feel better when we can touch and hold something that instinctively comforts us. Similarly, many overworked office workers like to use a rubber stress ball. This helps not just because of the effect of the tensing and relaxing, but also because of the simple experience of holding something. You can be as creative as you like in experimenting with this.

Working with Touch

You can use the following chart to record your impressions of the suggestions and experiments for using the power of touch to influence your state of mind. Often the impact of these experiments is very subtle, and you may notice their impact in your body, your personal habits, the way you speak, and how you relate to other people.

	If you have tried working with your sense of touch in this way, what was your initial experience of doing it?	If you have continued to work with this approach, what effects are you noticing?
Asking yourself how you feel—the tactile experience of your body.		
Working with your choice of clothing and footwear.		
Holding and touching objects.		

Refreshment

All our senses come into play when we have a meal, a snack, or a cup of tea or coffee with family or a friend. It's an honorable tradition. It meets our deep human need for refreshment, both nourishing us and revitalizing our spirit.

Often, when people are at work, they "grab a quick coffee" or eat a sandwich while working. This is part of our fast-food environment. The problem is that while we are just "getting a bite to eat," we are not really refreshing ourselves.

More and more people these days eat their meals alone. This is affecting family life and reducing simple human contact. That essential contact was part of the ancient tradition of taking tea together—a tradition that still lives on in some parts of the world.

What was important then—and is still true today—is the full sensory experience. That's why I recommend turning a meal or a drink with a friend or family member into an experience that encompasses all of your senses, if possible. For example, when making coffee with a filter, smell the freshly ground coffee. Fill the filter and place it in the glass bowl. Watch the coffee dripping though. Savor the wonderful aroma and the rich taste and warmth of the coffee as you share it with a friend. Your mind will calm down. You heart will warm. This is not time wasted. It is life refreshed.

Frequently Asked Questions

How can working with the senses help with strong feelings of anxiety, even panic? How can these simple methods help calm the nervous system?

We tend to think that our emotional experiences are more deeply ingrained in our beings than superficial sensory experiences. We associate our emotions with the mind and our sensory experiences with the body. In the qigong tradition, there is virtually no distinction between mind and body. Both are regarded as aspects of a single field of energy. Our energy field can be influenced just as easily and powerfully by our sensory experiences as by our emotions. However we direct our attention shapes our experience.

Do I need to follow these suggestions in any particular order?

No. The suggestions in this part of the book offer you a rich menu of possibilities. Everyone's experience of working with his or her senses will be different, just as it will be different for an individual on different days and at different times of the day. Please feel completely free to try any or all of these suggestions. Don't force yourself to work with something you don't want to. Enjoy experimenting with something that interests you.

Could experimenting with this kind of work increase my sensations of anxiety or fear?

Whenever you experiment with something new, there is an element of the unknown. If you have a long-standing habit of discomfort with uncertainty or fear of the unpredictable, then even the slightest change can bring up disturbing emotions. That can make these experiments all the more potent and helpful to you. For example, if you feel overwhelmed by deadlines and are worried you might lose your job by spending a minute listening to songbirds in the early morning, that might actually be the most powerful and beneficial moment in which to do exactly that.

Can I combine this use of the senses with the other exercises in this book?

Yes. All the suggestions for working with the senses can be combined with your practice of the qigong postures and movements. You can listen to music while standing still. You can feel your clothes and the air around you as you practice the movements. You can experiment with the scent of an aromatic oil. You can have a cup of tea or coffee before and after.

The Unseen Power of the Mind

In the many years in which I have taught in the West and treated people with a wide range of illnesses and injuries, I have noticed how skeptical they can be. Once I treated a gentleman who was suffering from back pain. He had been to many doctors and tried many expensive methods. He was lying on the floor when I treated him. After a few minutes of qigong massage, I told him he could stand up. He refused to believe me. I had to get his wife to help me convince him that his back pain was gone and that he could get up from the floor. He stood up and was able to move freely, without pain. Two days later, he called to say that he had booked himself into a clinic for a scan to find out whether my treatment had actually worked. He was going to spend thousands on it. I asked him, "Are you going to do this because you are in pain?" "No," he said, "because I am no longer in pain."

This skepticism affects our view of the world, but most importantly, our view of our own minds. We tend to have a fixed—and rather negative—view of the mind and of ourselves. How is it possible, we might ask, that we could use sight, sound, smell, taste, and touch to ease persistent anxiety? Is it simply a way of temporarily distracting us from our ongoing experience of pain?

The truth is that when we use our senses to their full extent, we are doing far more than distracting ourselves. We are using the deep resources of the mind—indeed, the full power of our entire energy system. Our senses are amazingly powerful. We can learn to tap into that power and use it for transformative, personal healing.

What makes this possible is something that is only now being validated by modern science, but which has been known to the qigong tradition for centuries. Physicians now refer to what is termed "the neuroplasticity of the brain." Put simply, it means that our brain activity, our thought patterns, and our sense of who we are are all far more fluid and flexible than we ordinarily think. The mind is a renewable resource. Its power is its freshness. We can tap into that freshness—instantly. That's what our senses are constantly inviting us to do.

The World Around Us

In the classical tradition, the four characters in this calligraphy are, from top to bottom: "heaven," "human," "join," and "one." This would conventionally be translated as "heaven and humanity joined together." However, there is a deeper way of understanding this.

The character for "heaven" is made up of four simple strokes, which represent, within the overall ideogram itself, "heaven," "earth," and "human being." Thus, compressed within the very first movements of the brush is an expression of the totality and inseparability of all existence. It is already joined together.

Nowadays we might say "galaxy" rather than "heaven." That also would convey both the breathtaking complexity and the beautiful simplicity expressed by this brushwork.

PART 5

Working with the Energy Around You

A Shimmering Net

The universe is a vast field of energy. The entire cosmos is a shimmering net of constant communication. Vibrations move through this net at inconceivable speed. Although our senses seem to perceive a world of separate forms, whatever we experience is, in fact, a pattern of energy.

To talk about the cosmos as an energetic spectrum is now commonplace in Western physics. But it was a fundamental tenet of Chinese science well before this millennium. The Chinese philosopher and naturalist Lu Yen wrote, "All substance and form is energy. It is yin and yang, the motion of the sun, moon and stars, everything that emerges and dissolves. It is the clouds, the mist, the fog, and moisture. The heart of all living beings, all growth and development is energy."

The original Chinese phrase that expressed our relationship to the rest of the universe was *chih chung*, sometimes translated as "magnetism." Just over two thousand years ago, in what is known as the Later Han Empire, natural scientists in China were exploring energetic attractions of all sorts. They established specific magnetic polarities, and their work has been described as "the greatest Chinese contribution to physics" (Needham, Wang, and Robinson 1962, 229). By the Tang Dynasty (618–906 CE), a compass was in use.

But the way in which *chih chung* was being explored took it far beyond the kind of magnetism in a fridge magnet. The meticulous observations of these early pioneers, who were also forming the basis of Chinese medicine, revealed that the human body also had magnetic properties. Latter-day scientists confirmed this through the presence of iron in the blood. We now know that our bodies are part of and are affected by the earth's magnetic field and that each of us has an energetic field extending beyond the visible limits of the body.

In these and many other ways, the energetic imprint of each human being is determined by the configuration of the force field of the universe at any one moment. This is why part 5 of the book opens with a calligraphy whose meaning is "the world around us." Is that world separate from us? Not at all. More accurately, we could say that we are that world—or that it is us. That is what is so beautifully and simply expressed by the four brushstrokes of the opening character of the calligraphy, which means "heaven" or "galaxy." Compressed within those strokes is the profound realization that heaven, earth, and humanity are one. We ourselves are the near and distant galaxies and the celestial rhythms that embrace us. This is the inner experience of qigong.

"This Immense, Living Field"

My sons are always showing me fascinating items they have found on the Internet. One day they showed me images from the Hubble Telescope, the most powerful telescope yet developed. Astronomers had trained it on a patch of sky that seemed completely empty, with no visible planets or stars. They said this patch of dark sky was no larger than a grain of sand held out at arm's length.

What the scientists found in that little point in space was the light from over three thousand galaxies. The telescope was receiving photons that had been traveling for more than thirteen billion years to reach Earth. The astronomers said that what they saw was "one of the most profound and humbling images in all of human history." Each one of those galaxies, which showed up on the telescope's receptor as little dots of light, contained hundreds of billions of stars. Later, they found another patch with ten thousand galaxies. They called it the Ultra Deep Field ("The Hubble Ultra Deep Field in 3D" 2009).

As I watched these images, they called to mind some of the oldest texts in the spiritual legacy of the East: magnificent Buddhist sutras describing infinite world systems with radiant light streaming throughout the cosmos. These poetic descriptions are now seen to be remarkably consistent with the unending discoveries of modern science (Ricard and Trinh 2001).

Sometimes, contemplating the vastness of the universe can make us feel anxious. We may feel small and of no value compared to the cosmos. It can fill us with loneliness and dread, reminding us of our fragility. But there is another way of looking at this. Not one in which we feel intimidated by the universe, but one in which we feel part of this immense, living field of sparkling energy.

In the Taoist tradition, which I have studied extensively, the human body is understood to be a small galaxy. The whole point of the inner practices of that tradition, which gave birth to qigong, is to connect each of our small galaxies with the rest of the universe, with the immense energy of the incalculable number of galaxies that surround us.

That is part of what we are able to do through our qigong practice. We train our own energy field in order to strengthen our sensitivity to and our connection with the vast energy field in which we live.

Environmental Energy

Places and environments are also fields of energy. You can sense this. Everyone has feelings about particular rooms and buildings. Those feelings are more than passing emotional states. You may be feeling anxious or suspicious about a location for a good reason. Our natural sensitivity tells us about the energetic qualities of locations. One place may feel welcoming, secure, or inspiring; another may feel threatening. Often, the feelings are health warnings. You just know a certain place is not a good one for you to be in.

In every moment of our lives we are picking up these kinds of messages. This shows that we are profoundly interconnected with our environments and that the energies that surround us shape our lives and our futures. Some messages warn us that if we sit in an exposed area, we may be approached from the rear without warning. Some tell us that our sleep may be disturbed if there is an open window over our bed. Others tell us where it feels best to have an intimate conversation.

Working with our own energy and the energy of our lives is the common experience of all humanity as we learn how best to live on this earth. It is our common home in space. Yet every person, every family, every home, every office, every day, and every place is different. Understanding and feeling this enables us to work with the energy of each situation as a fresh experience—and therefore with a spirit that is alert, accommodating, and spontaneous.

Qigong heightens our ability to sense the world around us. We become more alert, but we also feel more emotionally sensitive. You may be surprised by new feelings as you look at your home, your neighborhood, and your office with increased sensitivity. Another level of your natural intelligence is waking up.

Keen observation is important. That is why this is a workbook, with many charts that encourage you to reflect on your personal experience of qigong practice. There are questions about your physical and emotional experience, and many open-ended questions that simply invite you to ask yourself how you are reacting to the practices and exercises. This, too, is part of developing your sensitivity and appreciating it.

As that awareness develops on a personal level, it develops correspondingly on an environmental level. It's like having a new pair of glasses. You see so many things so much more clearly. You also become more curious about your own experience, about others, and about the amazing world around us. And that curiosity may lead to new and startling insights.

Home Energies

Whether we live in an apartment or a large house, whether we spend most of our time at home or travel frequently, the energy around us has an impact on our lives. Although our home is meant to be a place of nurture and support, many people can feel anxious or subtly disturbed at home. And it is well known that moving to a new home is a cause of high anxiety for many people.

From the point of view of our nervous system, there is one room in particular that has a pronounced effect—the bedroom—though other rooms have an impact as well. If we live in a one-room apartment, this effect is found in the part of the room where we sleep.

Most of us spend at least a third of our lives asleep in our bedrooms. This part of our lives is extremely important to us. We need to sleep well—deep, refreshing sleep. We need to dream—clear, regenerative dreams.

The bedroom has other roles as well. For many people, the bedroom is also one of the places of greatest intimacy in our lives. It is a place of privacy, and it is also a refuge. It is often here that we come for protection, for security and peace. We can "sleep" on our problems. We can curl up and turn away from the stress of the day—switching off the conscious activities of the brain and allowing the unconscious mind free rein.

We need to protect these precious hours of sleep and recuperation. If the bedroom is not a place of harmonious living, the consequences for our home lives can be devastating—and how often we have seen that devastation exported emotionally into the rest of our lives.

You want to have a bedroom that is as safe as possible, where your privacy is ensured, where the risk of intruders is minimal, and where the risk of accident is reduced. These qualities are all the more important to you when it is dark and you are asleep.

If you are buying or renting a new place to live, you should pay careful attention to the internal relationship between the bedroom and the rest of the space. Since the energies from the rest of the home enter the bedroom principally through the bedroom door, it is important to be particular about the areas of the home onto which the door opens. This may not seem all that important to you compared with other factors in choosing a new home—and the options you have may be limited—but remember that you will likely be spending such a great deal of your time in your bedroom that you will be profoundly affected by the energies that enter and circulate in that room.

If you are choosing a new home, it will be helpful to know a few basic elements from an energetic perspective. Energies can easily flow from one room to another if there is a direct line of movement through the doorways. In some homes, the entrance to the bedroom is directly in line with the front door. You are less likely to sleep soundly in such a home. Your nervous system will be most relaxed if your bedroom is an interior, private place. In other homes, the entrance to the bedroom is directly in line with the bathroom or kitchen. In those instances, it is necessary to make arrangements that will keep the bedroom free from odors, fumes, and noxious energies.

It may not always be possible to have a separate bedroom with a door. You may live in an open-plan home or a studio apartment, leaving you without a protected, quiet place of repose. If that's your situation, try to set up your living space so that the sleeping area is clearly defined and protected at night by a barrier, such as a bookcase or a screen.

Qigong at Home

Whether or not you are able to arrange your home taking all this into account, there is still one other thing that you can do: develop a daily qigong routine. It will make a difference in the quality of your life, both at home and away. Qigong is compatible with any other activity, like exercise or sports, and any sort of mind training, like meditation. Practicing a qigong routine every morning is like putting fresh batteries in your system before you start your daily activities. There is a sample routine in part 3.

Because you, your home, and anyone else who lives there are all fields of energy, the different energy patterns influence each other in a mutual, interdependent manner. We all know this from the simple fact that if one person is in a bad mood or acting in a disturbing way, he or she can upset everyone else and change the atmosphere in the home. Similarly, if you are regularly cultivating your life-enhancing energy and simultaneously calming your mind and nervous system, you will not only be less anxious and more emotionally resilient yourself, you will also have a beneficial effect on anyone you live with and the entire feel of your home.

Where You Work

The location of a shop, office, or factory is just as important to the well-being of the people who work there as the location of your home is to you and your family. Even if you don't have a choice about the location of your job, it is good to know if you are being exposed to helpful or potentially harmful energy there.

Urban environments can affect our nervous systems in numerous ways, which makes it all the more of a challenge to live healthily. It is not just our individual temperament that causes us to be anxious, experience high levels of stress, and have difficulty sleeping. These patterns can be heavily influenced by our environment.

If you work in a shop, a bank, or a restaurant, it is likely to be on a busy street or in a mall, grouped together with similar businesses to attract as many customers as possible. This means you will be exposed to a substantial volume of moving, volatile energy. You will inevitably be affected by that turbulence.

If you are an office worker, on the other hand, it is likely that you will not be exposed to the same kind of bustling energy that you would inside a busy store. In fact, if you are looking for an office location for yourself, it is best to look for a quiet corner in a busy area. Often, this means a side street adjacent to a major intersection or on the upper floors above the shops at street level. Although most office workers cannot choose the location where they work, there are still ways you can use your qigong practice to help you counteract the difficult conditions in which you may be working. We will look at some special features of office life in the next section, "Office Qigong."

If you work in a factory, you will know that they are, generally speaking, noisy places, and many generate fumes and waste. They need space, room to expand, and, usually, some open ground for off-site storage and transport. Since factories and light industrial complexes tend to be located in areas specially zoned for this kind of industry, your factory will likely be near other ones. The impact of the factories in the area is collective, which means that attention to health and safety and to each person's individual well-being is all the more important.

Being exposed to short periods of disturbed energy from a location is not necessarily a problem, even if it happens every day, as long as we are just dropping in. For example, the energy at a downtown intersection will be particularly disturbed. It might be a good location for stores that want to attract casual passersby, but if we were to try to live or work in that area, we would need to pay special attention to creating our own strong, protective energy field.

Office Qigong

Most modern offices network their computers so that employees can readily share information, use e-mail, and access the Internet. Computers are connected to the network by cable or Wi-Fi system. Cables usually run under the floor; a Wi-Fi system is all-pervasive.

All electrical items have electrical and magnetic fields. In the workplace, that includes the wiring for power, phone and network cables, fluorescent lighting, computers, and air conditioning units, as well as the large number of invisible electronic networks whose signals penetrate everywhere. Everyone in the office is surrounded by these fields. Some of these fields may be of low power, but even these add up to an environment of energetic disturbance that can negatively affect the health of people who work in it for sustained periods of time.

In the classical system of understanding energy patterns in which I was trained, electricity and electronic equipment like computers, cell phones, and personal sound systems are considered fire energy. Like a fire, the energy shoots upward and is radiant and powerful. It is warming, transformative, and communicative. It can also cause overheating, burning, and dryness; it can be all-consuming.

In traditional Chinese medicine, a serious imbalance of fire energy affects the heart and disturbs the nervous system. The results of prolonged exposure to the upward force and intense power of fire energy can affect your concentration. It can lead to headaches, anxiety, and loss of sexual appetite. You find yourself nervous, jumpy, and unable to relax.

If you work in this type of office, you will always be using up your own energy as your system tries to cope with the excess fire energy that envelops you. This, in turn, weakens your immune system and therefore your resistance to disease. If you find yourself spending long hours working in this type of environment and your employer is not alert to this problem, you should develop your own ways of coping with the effects of these disturbing energy fields.

Many practices offered in this book are helpful in counteracting the effects of fire energy. In part 3 you are introduced to the importance of connecting with the power of earth—"Taking Root" and the other practices. Remember that you can literally "ground" yourself by using these practices, the way electrical equipment is grounded.

All the suggestions for using the power of your senses in part 4 can be helpful in an office environment. For example, the practice of gazing into a blue- or green-tinted glass filled with water can be easily adapted for discreet use at your desk. If you rest your eyes on the glass from time to time, you will notice the effect this apparently simple practice has on your nervous system.

Take as many breaks as possible, to get out of the disturbing energy fields of the office. Literally go outside during breaks. Stand in the open air. This is a perfect time to practice the exercise "Coming Up for Air" in part 1. In meetings or at your desk, you can usually find a time when you can discreetly practice "Resting the Golden Ball," or a tensing and relaxing exercise like "Clenching and Relaxing."

Like many of my students, you may find that regular morning qigong sessions make a huge difference, setting you up for the day. Over time, it strengthens your immune system and creates a strong field of energy that can protect you from the disturbed vibrations of your work environment. You can begin with "Your Daily Routine" in part 3.

The problems caused by working at a computer keyboard are, by now, well known. These are associated with tension; in extreme cases, the strain leads to damage of the nerves in the wrist. In traditional Chinese medicine, the condition is relieved by massage, the application of herbs, and special exercises. To help prevent or relieve tension and pain in the hands, you can use the following simple qigong exercise for a few minutes before starting work at the keyboard or if you start to feel tired while working.

- Begin by sitting or standing for two or three minutes in the position "Holding the Golden Ball at Your Belly" (in part 2).

- Then raise your hands to elbow height and turn them so that your palms are turned down toward the floor. Your fingers are pointing straight ahead.

- Slowly raise your thumbs as far as you can without moving your other fingers. Hold for one second. Then lower them, pressing down as far as you can. Hold for one second. Then relax your thumbs.

- Now repeat this for each of the fingers on your hands—trying to raise and lower them in the same way, as far as you can without moving your other fingers.

These finger exercises not only help to remove the strain in your hands and improve the circulation of blood in your fingers, but are excellent stimulation for your brain. You will notice the effect that doing this has on your worries, anxieties, or other preoccupations.

Traveling Qigong

Many people feel anxious when traveling. Of course, there is also the excitement and arousal of traveling, but for many people, the panic of getting packed and off to the station or airport on time is very unsettling.

There are different ways you can use qigong when traveling. First, there is a way of working with your mind that may help you. Then, over these next few pages I show you a sequence of six exercises that will greatly help your energy, especially if you are traveling in cramped conditions or on an airplane.

Please take a look at the calligraphy at the beginning of the section "Earth" in part 3. It shows the Chinese character for the Tao. There is a long single brushstroke at the bottom that represents a raft, the sort of flat, simple craft used for centuries for navigating waterways—and still used today in some parts of the world. Just above it, at the left, is a small brushstroke that represents a person guiding the raft in the water. Picture yourself as that person. Your raft is floating in the currents of the water.

As you imagine this, you might close your eyes and feel that you are riding the current. You might sway a little as you do this. Try to feel that all the energy around you—the movements of your car or bus, the sounds and smells of the station or airport, the commotion of your family, the turbulence of the plane—are simply what you encounter as you balance on the raft, plying your oar in the water.

If you are not attracted to the image of a raft on water, you can imagine that you are being carried along in an old-fashioned bicycle taxi through the countryside. You feel the movement of the bike, the unevenness of the road, the air brushing against your face, and the feeling of the person who is riding the bike carrying you with them as you cycle along together.

While these images may be most useful when you are traveling, you can also use them at work or in other situations where the environment is somewhat unstable and makes you feel uneasy.

Giant Strides

This is the first of six qigong exercises that you can do while sitting to rouse your energy, calm your mind, and improve your circulation and well-being. I originally developed them for use on an airplane, but you can use them on any other long journey as well, in a bus or on a train.

Some seats make us slump so that our back is curved and our chest compressed. Try to sit up as best you can, but don't strain yourself too much.

Slowly lift one foot off the ground. As you raise your foot, stretch your toes up toward you as fully as possible. Breathe in as you raise your foot. Then slowly lower your foot as you breathe out.

Breathe in as you raise the other foot, again raising your toes up toward you as fully as possible.

Lift your feet eight times. Wait ten seconds. Then repeat the sequence two more times.

As you do this, imagine that you are taking huge strides over hills and mountains, like a giant. The movement is slow and powerful, your immense body covering miles with every step.

Bubbling Spring

This second traveling exercise focuses on one of the most potent acupuncture points on your body. Remain sitting comfortably in your seat, with your back as upright as possible.

Raise the heel of one of your feet, keeping the ball of your foot firmly on the floor. Then press the ball of your foot down into the floor. Use your calf muscles to get the pressure going straight down into the ball of your foot.

Breathe out as you press the ball of your foot down for a couple of seconds. Then relax, release the pressure on the ball of your foot, and breathe in. Lower your heel.

Then repeat with your other foot. Press and relax eight times, first one foot, then the other. Wait ten seconds. Then repeat the sequence two more times.

As you press down, you are activating the *yongquan* point on the sole of your foot, normally known as the "bubbling spring." This action sharply increases the flow of qi throughout your system, and the work done by your calf muscles speeds blood circulation.

Waves on the Rocks

In this, the third of the traveling exercises, try to sit up in your seat so that you do not strain your upper back. Place both your hands on your knees, so that your palms and fingers cover the entire area around the joints. Your fingers should curve over your knees so that your fingertips are well below your kneecaps.

Slowly rub your hands in smooth circles around the whole of your kneecaps. Your hands should circle around your knees starting with the inward aspect of each knee and circling around the front of the knee. The massage should be firm, but do not grip your knees.

Make thirty circles around the knees. If you have knee problems, do this massage as many times as you wish. Breathe naturally as you do it.

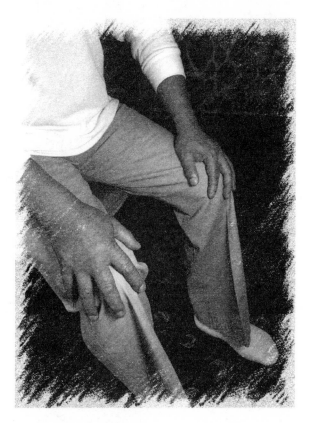

To get the right feeling for this exercise, imagine that your knees are large rocks at the edge of the sea. Your hands flow around them just like waves that roll in, cover the rocks, wash completely around them, and then recede. Use your fingertips to move firmly in and around the ridges and spaces below your kneecaps.

When you have finished, relax for a moment, with your hands resting on your knees or thighs.

Fearless Rider

In the fourth traveling exercise, begin by sitting in a resting position, with your back comfortably against your seat back. Your feet are flat on the floor.

Imagine that you are sitting in a saddle on the back of a powerful stallion. You are about to leap forward. As you feel the horse about to jump, you pull yourself forward fearlessly to ride upward with him. This forward pull takes place in the muscles of your buttocks, pelvis, and thighs. The shift in your hips automatically moves your back forward so that it is no longer touching the chair. As this happens, squeeze the muscles of your buttocks and thighs so that they are as taut as possible and you are fully sitting up. Breathe out as you come forward. Keep your upper body completely relaxed. .

Hold this forward position with the muscles of your buttocks and thighs tensed for a few seconds, without breathing in. Then gently release the pressure, completely relax, and sit back as you breathe in.

Sit up like this eight times. Wait ten seconds. Then repeat the sequence two more times

Crushing the Flanks

In the fifth traveling exercise, you are still riding the stallion. It is flying like the wind. To remain in position on its magnificent back, you need to grip its flanks tightly between your knees. As you crush the flanks, you imagine the full power of the horse carrying you with it.

Some people, when traveling, experience tremendous anxiety because they feel trapped, helpless, and at the mercy of whatever is going on in the airplane or on the train or bus. Their feelings of powerlessness affect their overall energy. This exercise can help shift those feelings, as it boosts your qi.

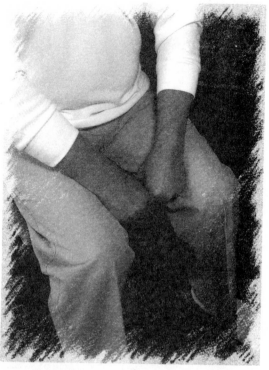

Sit forward, if you can. Fold both your hands into loose fists and turn them palms downward. Bring your fists together so that the thumbs and index fingers of each hand touch each other. Place your fists together between your knees.

Squeeze your knees together, pressing inward on your fists. Hold the squeeze for up to thirty seconds if you can. Breathe naturally as you do this.

Then relax. Wait ten seconds. Then repeat the sequence two more times.

Holding Two Forces

For the final traveling exercise, sit up as straight as you can in your seat. Slowly breathe out, letting your chest sink inward a little. Relax your shoulders.

Then, as you breathe in, bring your hands together in front of your chest and clasp them together.

Open your elbows outward so that your forearms form a right angle with your hands. Your palms are now vertical, pressing against each other.

Now press your palms firmly toward each other as you breathe out. Keep pressing for thirty seconds while breathing naturally. Alternatively, you may prefer to do this exercise by pressing your palms together for ten seconds while making one long exhalation.

Then slowly relax, keeping your arms in place. Breathe in slowly. Then repeat the pressing and relaxing, with synchronized breathing, two more times.

Your arms are like two forces relentlessly opposing each other. You feel the pressure they exert on each other, but your mind and body remain relaxed, so that the power of the two forces is calmly held by the entire field of your energy.

Experiencing Your Environments

At the beginning of part 5, you were introduced to ways in which you can experience and work with the energy of your home and work environments. This is a different approach to working with energy, but since you spend a great deal of time in your home and work environments, they have a sustained effect on you, your health, and your inner life.

Please use the following chart to record anything you notice about your home or workplace. You can also list any changes you have made or are planning to try. Remember that everyone's experience is different, so you need to pay careful attention to what you are sensing yourself. If you would like to have a checklist of sensations to help you with your personal review, you can use the "Quick Check" chart at the end of the introduction. You can use this chart for notes. If you find this helpful, you can continue to keep notes for yourself on a separate notepad.

Have you spent time sensing the different energies or feelings in different rooms or spots where you live? Were there any locations where the energy felt positive and supportive? Were there areas where you felt uncomfortable about the energy?
Did you consider the advice on arranging your bedroom that is given in the section "Home Energies"? Did you feel you wanted to make any changes? If you made changes, what was your experience of being in the bedroom after that?
Did you try any of the advice in the sections "Where You Work" and "Office Qigong" that might help you in your workplace? Have you noticed any effect?
If you have tried the six exercises for improving your energy circulation while traveling, what did you feel while doing them?
Have you noticed any effect on your nervous system when you imagine being surrounded by the energy of our galaxy and universe?

The Way of Nature

Nature is a living process of constant birth, death, and renewal. It is a process of perpetual rebalancing. It is never static, never the same. It is constantly coming to a beginning, over and over.

This is the deep truth embedded in the four characters of this calligraphy. At the very bottom, there are tiny brushstrokes. These represent fire—the cycle of creation and destruction through which life forever renews itself, as a forest does after a fire.

Taken together, the four characters of the calligraphy can be translated, "The method of the Tao is the process of following nature." Thus, its message is one of profound relaxation, the antidote to anxiety. You may be experiencing anxiety now, but this is not a permanent state, nor is it your nature. You will cycle through this, like life, again and again, always changing.

Practicing in Nature

As you make progress in your qigong training, you will become sensitive to the flow of energy within you and to the energy that surrounds you. You may be drawn to practice outdoors—in a garden, on a balcony, or in a local park. This is the way qigong has been practiced for centuries. You will feel refreshed by the air around you. However, it is not advisable to practice outdoors when it is windy or raining, and you shouldn't stand facing into direct sunlight, though sunlight on your back is beneficial. If you find it difficult to go outdoors for any reason, try to have a source of fresh air in the room where you do your exercises.

You can enhance your sensitivity to the natural world and derive immense benefit from it by learning to practice with a tree.

This photo was taken when I went to Muir Woods, the marvelous redwood forest in northern California. The power of the natural energy in the woodland is wonderfully invigorating.

Trees are among the great powerhouses of nature, and the energy they radiate is extremely powerful. The presence of trees is a tremendous support for your practice, stabilizing and calming you with their protective power.

If you would like to try this practice, look for a tree that exudes a sense of strength, power, and well-being. It need not be a huge tree, but you should have the feeling that its energy is healthy.

Stand a few feet away from the tree in any of the qigong positions. For this practice (which is slightly different than what you see in the photo), please make sure you face the tree.

Imagine that there is a circuit of energy that extends from the crown of the tree down to the top of your head. It continues through your body down to your feet, then down into the earth, where it connects with the roots of the tree. The circuit continues back up through the tree until it begins to circle down through the top of your head again.

As you imagine the tree's energy coming in through the top of your head, breathe in. As it goes from your feet back into the tree, breathe out.

As you stand, allow your mind to rest on this continuous circuit. Experienced practitioners report feeling the mutual cycle of energy between them and the tree as they relax into the experience.

You can do any or all of the qigong practices in this book outdoors. If you start your day with a little routine, like the one at the end of part 3, doing all or part of your routine outdoors can give your energy a real boost and help your nervous system recover from any overnight worries, sleeplessness, or strain.

Your Senses and Your Mind in Nature

Practicing qigong outdoors is an excellent opportunity to use your senses and your mind to help you with your anxiety. Feel the air on your face, listen to the sounds of the trees, smell the grass and the flowers. Breathe freely in a relaxed way.

If there is a stream in the park or woodland, you can spend a few moments looking at the running water. If you see a stone in the water, observe how the water flows around and past it in an unending current. Try thinking of yourself as a smooth stone, standing in the current of all your anxieties and difficulties. They flow around you as you remain unmoving in the stream. Try to form a clear image of the water flowing past the stone in your memory, so you can use it later. Being a stone in the water doesn't mean that you become unfeeling or cold as a person. It simply means that you take your place in the flowing current of your life but are not swept away by it.

Don't confuse this outdoor practice with meditation. You can talk to your friends or anyone you meet in the park. If you like to sing to yourself, please do. But please take this opportunity not to use headphones to listen to music or anything else. This is a time to appreciate nature just as it is.

Your Natural Experience

You have been taking your qigong practice out into nature. Outdoor practice enables you to feel more expansive, to do the exercises in the open air and to spend time making a connection with trees—some of nature's most powerful energy transformers. You can do other qigong practices outdoors as well. In the chart below are some suggestions for practices that you can try outdoors. Follow your own preferences.

It is very helpful to keep track of your experience of doing qigong. You are the only person who can feel what is happening as you do this and how it is affecting your anxiety patterns. If you would like to have a checklist of sensations to help you with your personal review, you can use the "Quick Check" chart at the end of the introduction. If you find this helpful, you can continue to keep notes for yourself on a separate notepad.

	If you have tried doing this, what was your initial experience of doing it?	If you have continued to do this, what effects are you noticing?
Practicing "Coming Up for Air" and the standing exercises in part 1 to get you started outdoors.		
Creating an energy circuit with a tree.		
Practicing "Your Daily Routine" (part 3) outdoors.		

The Two Poles

As you develop your practice of qigong, your hands become increasingly powerful conduits of energy. They are like the two poles of a magnetic field—at any one time, one of these poles is positive, the other is negative. As your sensitivity increases and your qi becomes more and more powerful, you can feel the invisible current running between your palms.

There are numerous healing applications of this current. Your hands can be used in exactly the same way that magnets are used in magnet therapy. By placing your hands at different points on the body, the current passes through the body from one palm to the other.

Before performing the qigong massage techniques described on the following pages, you need to ensure that there is a strong flow of qi to your hands.

Stand in the position "Holding the Golden Ball at Your Belly" for at least five minutes. If possible, lower yourself down a little farther than usual. Your upper body should be relaxed. Spread your fingers amply apart.

When you have completed your standing, rub your palms rapidly together for at least thirty seconds to warm them. Clap your hands together about a dozen times to bring your inner qi to the surface of your palms. You are then ready to work.

You will be using your hands like two magnetic poles of yin and yang energy. There are many ways of using this energy, including as first aid in some situations. If you have an accident, such as bumping some part of your body or stumbling and wrenching your ankle, you can apply your palms on either side of the affected area. This calms the nervous reaction and steadies the entire area, and—depending on what has happened to you—you may well find that it can relieve your pain and help reduce swelling.

You can imagine that the part of your body that is held between your hands is a small planet, like our own earth. The energy field between your hands is like the energy of the galaxy that surrounds the earth and sustains its biosphere. You are using the flow of your qi as a field of warmth, support, and nurture.

In our tradition, this use of qi is often referred to as "natural medicine." The great Taoist sage Zhuangzi (also transliterated "Chuang Tse"), who lived about 2,500 years ago, wrote about this: "The three treasures of vitality, energy, and spirit experience a daily flourishing of life and fill the whole body, so that great medicine can be expected to be produced naturally."

This "natural medicine" is one of the accomplishments of qigong practice. As you mature in your practice, the quality and power of your inner energy changes. What might have been a somewhat weak, irregular, unstable flow of energy becomes fuller, more constant, and unending—less like a stream, more like a broad river. This enhanced flow of energy can be used for some forms of self-healing and helping others.

I have done this kind of healing massage for most of my working life. I began with a clinic in Hong Kong after my training as a traditional herbalist and bonesetter, and I have since treated countless people in my centers in London and Piedmont, California. I have trained a number of my senior students in this method as well. They like to report their experiences to me, especially if they have been able to use their qi successfully in emergencies. One of them told me of such a success.

> I was walking on an uneven pavement and suddenly stumbled. My foot slipped off a loose paving stone, and my foot twisted to one side. I landed sharply on the side of my foot, pulling and twisting my ankle at the same time. The shock went right through my body. I immediately stopped and began rubbing my palms together. When they were warm, I knelt down and held my ankle between them. Then, after a little while, I gave the whole area a good, strong massage with my palms. I wasn't sure what the effect would be. When I stood up, I found I could place all my weight on the affected leg. Then I slowly moved my ankle. It was tender. I took a few steps and felt I could move it and continue walking. When I looked at my ankle that evening, there was no swelling.

If you have not practiced zhan zhuang qigong regularly, have been practicing incorrectly, or have only been practicing for a relatively short period of time, you should not expect to achieve miraculous results. But if you practice regularly and experience the sensations of the energy current between your palms, you can use your qi in this way and in the applications described in the following pages.

Neck and Face Self-Massage

You can use your energy for healing and calming self-massage. Your nervous system will respond wonderfully to a soothing qi massage of your neck and face, which will remove tension in your neck and bring radiant energy to your face.

First, place your hands together and rub them together vigorously for a little while. Try to make sure that your fingers and fingertips are also rubbing against each other.

This automatically brings more qi to your hands. Most people experience the effect immediately: your hands and fingers become warm. Even if you do not experience increased warmth, your energy is there.

Then rub your hands back and forth over the back of your neck. This helps to clear blockages and stiffness that impede the flow of energy to the brain and nervous system.

You can also give yourself a little "qi facial" this way. Gently rub your hands over your eyes, ears, and face, as if washing yourself. Try feeling the effect of holding your palms over your closed eyes for a few seconds—and then over your ears.

Soothing Your Back

Anxiety and other inner torment is one of the most common causes of backache. This painful condition affects millions of people. If you suffer from it, you may be able to give yourself some relief with a qigong massage. This should not be mistaken for a cure for back pain, especially if you are suffering from an injury to your back, a pinched nerve, or a chronic condition. But the warming flow of qi will help soothe you, lower your level of anxiety, and offer you some relief.

First rub your palms together to stimulate your qi. Curl your fingers into open fists, as if you were holding an egg in each hand.

Place your open fists in the small of your back so that the curve between your thumb and your index finger rests in the soft flesh just above your hips. You are not using the whole of your hand, just the curve between your thumb and index finger. Then use your open fists to massage those two spots in your back for as long as you wish.

Easing Headaches

There are many causes of headaches. Some are the result of accidents and injuries, which require specialized treatment. But many ordinary headaches are caused by a blockage of qi in the area of the neck and shoulders, which affects the supply of blood and oxygen to the brain. You can use the following sequence for relief.

Begin by stimulating the flow of qi to your palms using the "Two Poles" method.

Then work with the tips of two or three fingers on each temple. Make smooth circles around the area of the temples, pressing gently inward. Make thirty-six small circles.

Then run your fingers along both sides of the head, from the temples to behind the ears and down to the base of the skull at the back of your neck. Repeat this flowing motion six times.

Then work the tips of two or three fingers on either side of the back of the neck, below the base of the skull. Make thirty-six small circles, pressing gently inward as you move. Finish by "washing" your head and face with firm, smooth, circular movements for about a minute.

Energy Circuit

Another way to work with the living energy of the world around you is to create an energy circuit with a partner. I recommend you do this with a family member or a good friend—someone with whom you have a warm, supportive connection already. It is not necessary for both of you to have experience with qigong, but one of you should at least be experimenting with the practices in this book. If both of you are doing some daily qigong practice, of course, the effect will be even stronger.

Stand facing each other. It is best if your feet are shoulder-width apart. Move your arms so that they are positioned at a 45-degree angle to the side, level with your waist. The palm of your right hand faces down; the palm of your left hand is turned upward.

Hold your right hand over the other person's left hand, with your palm facing down over your partner's palm. Your two palms are facing each other. Leave some space in between your palms, as if you were holding an orange between them.

Your energy will naturally create a circuit through your hands. Breathe naturally. Just stand for a few minutes like this, breathing naturally and relaxing.

Many people ask me exactly what path the energy takes. You can think of it traveling from the palm of the first person's right hand (which is facing downward) into the palm of the other person's left hand. The right hand is passing energy into the left and the left is taking it. The energy simultaneously makes a circuit through your two bodies and continues through the connection of the other two hands.

You can also work with this energy circuit sitting down. Simply arrange yourselves so that you are facing each other and create the circuit with your outstretched palms. If one person is unable to stand up for any reason, that person can remain seated while the other stands.

If you have trouble figuring out the hand positions, please look carefully at the two hands in the foreground of the picture, which shows the correct position with one person's right hand on top, palm facing down, and the other's left hand underneath with the palm turned upward. The photo also shows the space between the hands. If you get one set of your palms properly aligned, then you can simply copy that (in reverse position) for the other set of palms. The photo also shows that the fingers of your hands are gently spread apart, but they are not tense.

There are many ways we can use and benefit from an energy circuit like this. If you are feeling anxious, just ask your partner to stand with you for a minute or two. In my experience with many students, even those two minutes can be extremely helpful. You will find that the energy of anxiety is neutralized.

What happens if both people are feeling anxious? Your energy circuit will carry your anxiety along with it. The way energy flows, the weaker, most disturbed anxiety energy will flow downward toward the earth and dissipate into the ground. That will leave a strong circuit of supportive energy flowing between you.

Experiencing Energy Work

Have you tried the various forms of energy work that you were introduced to in this part of the book? These include energy massages ("The Two Poles"), as well as working with another person to create a shared energy field ("Energy Circuit"). It's important to pay attention to the effect of these practices, so that you can learn from them and develop your ability.

It can also be wonderful to ask your partners about their experience, so there is space on this chart for that too. Remember that everyone's experience is unique—not better or worse than anyone else's. If you find this helpful, you can continue to keep notes for yourself on a separate notepad.

What did you experience as you followed the instructions for "The Two Poles"?
If you tried giving yourself a qigong neck and face massage, what effect did it have?
If you experimented with giving yourself a qigong back massage, how did you feel, during and afterward?
If you had a headache and tried using the qigong method "Easing Headaches," what happened?
If you experimented with creating an "Energy Circuit" with a partner, what did you each experience?

Inner Growth—A Nine-Month Review

Please come back to the following chart on the date that you entered in the box "date nine months from now" in the "Growing from Within" chart at the end of part 1. Answer these questions without looking back to see what answers you gave nine months ago. Then you can compare your answers and reflect on your experience.

It doesn't matter if you have maintained a regular qigong practice or followed any of the recommendations in this book. Life is a process of constant change, and it is always helpful to take a few minutes to review your experience. Please remember that every person is unique. These charts are meant for your personal, private use. Please treat them like an intimate conversation with yourself.

Date today:	Date on which you completed the "Growing from Within" chart:

How is anxiety showing up in your life these days?
Do you see any common patterns in the anxiety you feel at home, in your workplace, or elsewhere?
How frequently do you experience fear or panic?
If you feel overwhelmed and have feelings of despair, how are you coping with them?
If you have been using this workbook to help you with your anxiety, have your family or friends noticed any differences in you?

How would you describe the pattern of your energy these days?

Do you experience much fatigue?

If you have been using this workbook, have you noticed any changes in the tension in your body?

What is your normal pattern of sleep now?

How do you feel when you wake up in the morning now?

Are you experiencing any digestive problems?

What are the main ways you have used this workbook to help with your anxiety?

What is the main challenge you have faced in the qigong exercises you have experimented with?

Frequently Asked Questions

Are there any times or conditions in which it is not good to practice qigong outdoors?

It is best to practice qigong outdoors during the day. If you are an early riser and want to start practicing before dawn, that is fine, especially if you are able to arrange to include the sunrise in the period of your practice. Normally, you should try practice with sunlight striking your back. Sun energy connects with an important acupuncture point in the small of your back, known as *mingmen (ming men)*, the "gate of fire." Facing strong sunlight can make you squint and tense up, thus impeding the flow of energy. It is best not to practice outdoors if it is misty, foggy, or rainy. Damp conditions can also impede the flow of energy.

What happens if dogs or other animals see a person "standing like a tree"?

Animals have a natural attraction to strong energy. Dogs and other pets, whether at home or outdoors, may take an interest in a person doing qigong. If they know you, they may wish to lie down near you or be in the area where you are practicing. If they don't know you, they might run over to you to check you out. If a dog you don't know is barking or jumping up and down, it is best to remain still and not make any sudden movements, in case this is startling. If you want to move away, lower your arms to a normal position and walk calmly and slowly on. Once when I was in a park with one of my students, a squirrel ran up his leg and sat for a while on his shoulder. We had a good laugh about how he was doing quite well at standing like a tree.

What should I do if there are no changes I can make to the conditions in my home or workplace?

Sometimes it is simply impossible to make physical changes to your environment. In that case, it is important to realize that regular, consistent practice of qigong creates a strong energetic field that not only helps you internally, but also acts as a sphere of protection around you. This is sometimes referred to as the "aura" and is what can be seen using bioelectrography, also known as Kirlian photography, which picks up the electrical field around a person. In the section on your workplace ("Where You Work," in part 5), I give specific suggestions to help you cope with the intense energy of many contemporary offices.

Can you pick up other people's illnesses by practicing qigong or exchanging energy with them?

If you are in the same room as a person with a cough or a cold, you can pick that up through the normal route of physical infection. That's natural and can happen whether you are practicing qigong with them or not. But the practice of qigong has a positive effect on your immune system and helps you bounce back faster if you do have any kind of illness or injury. So the most important thing is to try to establish a good daily foundation of refreshing your energy. If you do that, you will be at less risk of becoming ill, no matter how you come in contact with illnesses.

Does This Really Work?

The only person who can answer this question is you. Personal experience is the basis of the qigong tradition. Qigong has always been handed down from person to person. And the reason it has been passed on is that one person after another found that it really worked for them. But if you don't find it helpful, or if you don't see a way of fitting it into your life, please don't worry. There are other methods of working with energy, and since energy is all around us, you will never be without it.

What I have found is that people from all walks of life can find ways to fit a little qigong into their lives, and they find it helpful. That is why I have told their stories throughout the book. You may have noticed that my students come from a range of backgrounds: teaching, medical care, law, business, real estate, computing, international relations, and community service—and add to that list my own early days as a police officer.

Some of my students are artists. They too put qigong to use in their work. One is an opera singer. She told me, "Zhan zhuang qigong has extended my capacity. The change is fundamental: you can hear the difference. I am stronger, breathe deeper, and project my voice farther. Zhan zhuang changed my awareness of my inner space. I couldn't have learned this just from taking singing lessons."

I am not asking you to believe me. I am offering you the possibility of trying it out for yourself. Then you can decide whether it works or not.

A Living Fire

If you want to keep a fire alive, you need to ensure that there are burning embers that will stay alight until dawn. That is the meaning of the first of these four characters.

The second character represents the fire itself.

The last two characters express the idea of "passing the baton." In a relay race each runner carries the baton and then carefully hands it on to the next teammate.

Read together, these four characters describe the notion of "lineage." A lineage is a living fire. Like the Olympic flame, it is carefully kept alight and then is passed from hand to hand. That is clear from the last three characters. The first one, however, adds a warning. You can admire a fire that is already burning and decide to start your own. But that is a different fire. It is not the same as keeping the power of the original fire alive.

The Lineage

The practice of cultivating human energy has been passed down from master to student in a lineage that stretches back some twenty-seven centuries. Like all forms of energy, it can be used in a variety of ways. From those earliest days, there has always been a distinctive stream of this tradition that has used energy to relax and nurture the human being, both mentally and physically. My own master was fond of recounting the thousands of years of history through which the art of qigong has developed. It is thanks to those many generations of masters and students that it is possible for me to share with you today the benefits that qigong offers for alleviating anxiety.

Two of the earliest books about qigong are a medical treatise and one of China's most famed books of philosophy. *The Yellow Emperor's Classic of Internal Medicine* (*Huang Ti Nei Ching*), the world's most influential medical text, appeared some 2,400 years ago. In it, the court physician tells the emperor: "The sages were tranquilly content with nothingness and the true vital force accompanied them always. Their vital spirit was preserved within."

The *Tao Te Ching*, by Laozi—one of the most widely read and influential books in the course of human civilization—says, "By standing alone and unchanging, you will find that everything comes to you and the energy of the cosmos will never be exhausted." "Standing alone and unchanging" was Laozi's way of describing the practice through which we have come to understand the full power of the universe.

The cultivation of internal energy was developed as part of Taoism. It included the practice of remaining completely still in fixed positions. The Taoist philosopher Zhuangzi tells us that the sages of old were "still and unmoved....Their breathing came deep and silent." Their "minds were free from all disturbance…forgetting everything." They were "open to everything and forgot all fear of death." In the text, a disciple tells his master, "I am making progress." "What do you mean?" asks the master. "I sit and forget everything…becoming one with the great void in which there is no obstruction."

Buddhist thought and practice also influenced the development of the qigong tradition. The development of "one-pointedness" of mind (that is, the ability of the mind to be clearly focused) in the Buddhist tradition made a major contribution to the cultivation and application of qi in the human energy system.

The practices of qigong were passed down through the centuries in a lineage that was largely kept secret. It was not until the twentieth century that this heritage was shared openly in China and brought to the West.

The person who unlocked these secrets for the modern world was Grand Master  Wang Xiang Zhai. Born in 1885 in the Shenxian district of Hebei province, he suffered from poor health as a child. His father was determined to improve his son's physical condition and sent him for training under his uncle, Master Guo Yun Sin, who lived in his village. From Master Guo he learned the secret discipline of zhan zhuang qigong. After his master's death, the young Wang spent ten years traveling throughout China, meeting and studying under the great masters of his day.

By the mid-1940s, he was ready to teach and pass on the fruits of what he had learned and moved to Beijing, where he was soon recognized as a master of extraordinary wisdom and prowess. His accomplishment was vast. From his humble origins as a boy suffering from asthma that left him severely weakened, he became a pivotal figure in the qigong tradition, bringing many of its most profound secrets out from centuries of secrecy into the modern world.

In the course of his studies, Grand Master Wang delved deeply into the spiritual heritage of Chinese culture, immersing himself in the wisdom of the Taoist and Buddhist traditions. Grand Master Wang composed poems to guide his many students on the path of qigong practice—attempting to convey in words the inner experience of this art.

You who wish to master this art, begin by standing still.
Breathe deeply, undisturbed, like air among the clouds.
Your spirit and your bones are being tempered in this forge.
Hold still, unwavering.
This wisdom will suffuse your being, ceaselessly.

Grand Master Wang broke new ground by challenging the traditional secrecy of qigong instruction. He taught openly. "Knowledge should not be hidden away like a secret," he said. "It belongs to all humanity."

One of the earliest students of Grand Master Wang was a young man who had studied Western medicine and was serving as a dentist at the Ten Lu (Railway) Hospital. His name was Yu Yongnian.

After nine years of study and practice under Grand Master Wang, Yu began introducing aspects of zhan zhuang qigong as treatment for chronic diseases at his hospital. His initial successes were such that a major medical conference was held at the Beijing Shoudong San Hospital three years later, in 1956, to introduce the zhan zhuang system to hospitals throughout China.

After the Cultural Revolution, Professor Yu published groundbreaking books on zhan zhuang. The first edition of *Zhan Zhuang for Health* came out in February 1982 (Beijing: Educational Publishers). By April a second edition of 120,000 copies was issued, and by 1987 a further 294,500 copies had been printed. A limited edition of his next book, *Application of Zhan Zhuang for Health*, was published in Beijing in 1989, and in the same year a further work on zhan zhuang qigong was issued by Cosmos Books in Hong Kong.

Professor Yu became the world's leading authority on zhan zhuang qigong, was on China's National Qigong Research Council, was a former consultant to the American-Chinese Qigong Research Group, and was honorary chairperson of the Da Cheng Chuan Zhan Zhuang Chi Kung Research Groups (Europe).

"Taking Tea with My Master"

Almost as soon as I was introduced to the art of qigong, I realized that it was far more powerful than anything I had ever learned before. I wanted to go directly to the source and learn as much as I could. The world's leading authority on the zhan zhuang tradition of qigong was a master in Beijing, Professor Yu Yongnian. I wanted to learn directly from him.

Sadly, this was at the time of the Cultural Revolution in China. It was a very dangerous period. Since I was from Hong Kong (still a British colony at that time), I would be viewed as a foreigner, and traveling to Mainland China to visit Professor Yu could create difficulties for him. So I wrote to him; luckily, this was possible. After we had exchanged many polite letters, I told him I wanted to study with him. He replied that I should come to take tea with him at his home.

Even though having a foreign visitor could place him in danger, he welcomed me. He served me tea in the traditional way, and we had a polite conversation. Then it was time for me to leave. As I left his home, he said nothing about whether I could be his student, but he told me, "Please take tea with me again."

I ended up visiting him three times, and only at the end of our third visit did he say he would start sharing some ideas with me. When I returned the next time, he said to me, "Now you will need to start all over again at the very beginning." In this way, I became his devoted student. Teaching me was not a decision he took lightly—that's why he had wanted to see me again and again. He wanted to observe me, listen to the way I spoke, watch the way I handled a teacup, get a feeling of my own attitude toward him, and examine what I had already learned. At the same time, we were strengthening the connection between us—the invisible channel that would carry centuries of wisdom and experience forward to the future.

I owe him a huge debt of gratitude, because he taught me in a very deep and meaningful way. What he transmitted was something that can only be passed on through the power of lineage.

Lineage is how a truly authentic art is handed down and kept alive, transmitted in a very personal way. That is why I want you, dear reader, to know about the centuries of human learning through which this art has been developed and passed on. Of course, reading a book is not the same as learning directly from a lineage holder. But now that you have started to take an interest in this art, if you read and respect the stories, photos, and statements in these pages—which I have put together to give you a sense of our shared history—I hope you will have a feeling of what it might be like to start taking tea with a master.

I first heard about Professor Yu in the 1980s. It was not possible for me to meet him—I could only write to him, because China was still in the grip of the Cultural Revolution. Later, I was finally able to travel to Beijing and was accepted as one of his students. Even though I now live and teach in the West, I continue to respect the classical tradition of the master-student relationship and, until his death in 2013, returned regularly to China to practice with Professor Yu and learn from his lifetime of experience in this art.

The calligraphy on this page is a gift that I received from Professor Yu. A literal translation is "Follow the Tao, day by day, less and less." It means that as we continue practicing qigong correctly every day, we gradually experience less and less of whatever troubles us. Less anxiety, less tension, less pain. It is like polishing something precious—slowly the accumulated dust and dirt are removed and the original quality is revealed.

You may sometimes see "qigong" spelled "chi kung," though the pronunciation is always the same. So why the difference in spelling? It reflects two ways of transliterating Chinese into English. "Chi kung" is the spelling using the Wade-Giles system of transliteration, which was developed by two British diplomats serving in China in the nineteenth century. Wade-Giles was widely in use throughout most of the twentieth century. Most of the Chinese masters who preserved the classical Chinese arts during the often catastrophic turbulence of that century used the Wade-Giles system when writing their teachings in English. I grew up using that system, and all my books have used it. Nowadays, however, the newer pinyin system of transliteration is used in China, having been adopted by the government. This spelling is much more common in the United States, and so I have used it in this book. To help readers familiar with the earlier system of transliteration, I have included that in parentheses on first reference. I have kept most of the titles of works or names that used the earlier system in that form.

"Pervading Anxiety"

One of my students is a commercial program manager. When he first came to see me, he told me, "I am experiencing pervasive anxiety." He had done some martial arts when he was younger and decided some kind of internal energy practice might help him with his inner distress. Later, he told me how he was doing.

My anxiety has decreased substantially. Once I started learning from you, even when my anxiety arises I am more able to just observe it, which allows it to pass more easily, without me becoming embroiled in a futile battle against fear.

I find that through practicing qigong, I am able to reach a state of peace, calm, and serenity that is unobtainable by any other means of meditation, relaxation, or even sleep. This is after having tried various meditation and relaxation techniques over a period of around six years.

After practicing qigong, it feels like I have just had a shower. People often comment on how fresh and relaxed I look, which does not happen if I have not practiced for a while!

You can pass through the whole cycle of emotions, from resistance, anger, fear, pain, and elation....You learn to let go and observe the experiences and sensations, which is good practice and training for the many obstacles that appear in daily life.

Qigong is different from many other systems, because you are not "trying" to do anything. In other systems, you often have to try to send energy here or there, or you focus on your breathing. This often either leads to the energy only being in your head or causes tension from the "trying." The zhan zhuang system seems to be more natural, as it seems to work on the basis that if you relax, the energy does the work for you, and your mind and body eventually end up where they need to be.

Even after practicing for a short period of time, it is possible to quickly and easily obtain a state of consciousness where all of your worries disappear while strengthening your body and spirit. Over time, this sense of well-being also spreads into your daily life.

If You Are Opening the Book Here and Looking for Help in a Hurry

People tell me that they are drowning. They may be drowning in their work, the pressure of deadlines, or the overwhelming demands and conflicts in their lives. They need to come up for air.

There's a powerful qigong practice for this. It's called "Coming Up for Air." You can try it for yourself: there are photos and clear instructions in part 1 of this book.

"Qigong," pronounced "chee gung," literally means "internal energy work." The system has been in use for twenty-seven centuries and is part of China's medical heritage. It helps the flow of vital energy in the body.

Don't worry about the theory. You can read that later. This book is designed for practical use. You can pick out anything you would like to try. It has many illustrations and is designed to be readable at a glance, so you can rest the book beside you and follow the instructions. Many of the exercises in this book are designed to address particular problems.

If you start worrying first thing in the morning—before you even get out of bed—or if you suffer from insomnia, go to the exercises, "Overwhelmed, Lying Down" and "In the Middle of the Night" in part 3. You can do these deep practices lying on your back, in bed or on the floor, in the morning or at night.

If you suffer from panic attacks or constant anxiety that makes you tense up all the time, go to "Tensing and Relaxing" in part 2. You can also try "Clenching and Relaxing." You clench and stretch your hands, using your muscles to trigger a relaxation effect in your nervous system, similar to using a stress ball.

If you want to find out in depth how to use this ancient health system to handle your anxiety and develop your inner strength, I recommend you read the introduction and then start with the exercises in part 1. You can use the charts to keep track of how you are doing.

If, however, you're eager to jump right in, just do that. You can open the book at any page and try whatever exercise pops up there. They are all designed to help you work with your anxiety.

About the Author

Master Lam has helped millions on the road to health. He has devoted his life to the study of qigong and the other healing arts of Chinese culture. From an early age he learned under some of the greatest masters of his time, in Hong Kong, Taiwan, and China. He has been teaching in the West since 1975, opening up the secrets of Chinese health care through his books, videos, workshops, and classes.

Master Lam is a lineage holder of the classical zhan zhuang qigong tradition established by Grand Master Wang Xiang Zhai. This is widely known as "Standing Like a Tree," an art Master Lam first introduced to the West in his groundbreaking book *The Way of Energy*. It is this time-tested system for regenerative health that lies at the heart of this workbook.

Master Lam is also the founder of Lam-style Tai Chi Chuan, developed to enable people in the West to learn and practice the principal foundational movements of tai chi chuan.

Born in Hong Kong at the end of the Second World War, Master Lam first studied under masters such as Lung Tse-Cheung, a disciple of Grand Master Hu Yue-Chang, known throughout China as "the king of Iron Palm." He was trained in the arts of Choy Lee Fut, Northern Shaolin Kung Fu, and Iron Palm, as well as tai chi.

He then studied Chinese medicine, becoming a qualified bonesetter and herbalist, and opened a school and clinic in Hong Kong. At this stage in his career, he was introduced to a master trained in the tradition of Grand Master Wang Xiang Zhai, who had opened up the world of zhan zhuang qigong to the public. Master Lam went on to study in Beijing under Professor Yu Yongnian, a grand master of the art of zhan zhuang. Professor Yu, who recently died, was the world's leading authority on this system of qigong; his books are widely used in China.

Master Lam first settled in London in the mid-1970s. He became the first person officially recognized by the Inner London Educational Authority to teach the art of tai chi, thus opening up this field for formal acceptance in education. He opened a clinic in London and established both the Lam Association of Cultural Arts and the Zhan Zhuang Chi Kung Research Group (Europe), with members in nearly a dozen countries. During this time, he demonstrated the power of his art by using qigong to heal himself after a near-fatal accident and a life-threatening illness.

In 2009, Master Lam explored teaching and offering healing treatments in the United States. He settled in Piedmont, California. Now he divides his time between Europe and North America, giving private teaching, public classes and workshops, and professional seminars, as well as offering KTL Therapy, a synthesis of all his life experience named for the members of his family who work with him to provide it.

Master Lam is the author of a range of books on tai chi, qigong, and feng shui. Among his most widely read works, published in over a dozen languages, are *Step-by-Step Tai Chi* and his qigong trilogy, *The Way of Energy*, *The Way of Healing*, and *The Way of Power*. He is well-known as the presenter of the ten-part Channel Four series *Stand Still—Be Fit*, which you can watch on Master Lam's website (see the section "Master Lam on Film" for more).

Healing and Training with Master Lam

Master Lam offers personal training, public classes, workshops, and professional seminars. He also offers qigong healing treatments. He is based in Piedmont, California, and in London, England. He travels widely throughout the year.

It is important to understand that the practices and recommendations in this book are based on a lifetime of study and practice. You are more than welcome to experiment with them yourself. Using this book, while beneficial to you personally, does not constitute an authorization to teach qigong to others, to present yourself as a student of Master Lam, or to publish this information in books or on websites. If you would like to take your training further or explore how to share it with others who might benefit, please contact Master Lam to discuss this and find out about the training and worksops he offers.

Healing Treatments

Master Lam has a lifetime of experience in healing a wide range of disorders. Through his own years of research and experience, Master Lam now offers a qigong healing system known as KTL Therapy. It is based on accumulated research into the healing properties of countless herbs, the physical structures of the body, and the pathways through which our internal energy moves. This system has proven to be effective in helping people with many illnesses and injuries. Testimonials are published on his website, http://www.lamkamchuen. org. The site includes a list of conditions that can be helped by this therapy. These include dorsalgia (back pain), whiplash, sciatica, joint dislocation, accidents and sports injuries, and neck and shoulder pain, as well as hip, knee, and ankle pain.

If you would like to make an appointment for treatment with Master Lam, please contact him. His phone number in the United States is 1-510-666-7889. His international headquarters is in London, England: +44 207 261 9049. His e-mail address is hq@lamassociation.org.

Personal Training

If you would like to study privately with Master Lam, please contact him for an appointment. His phone number in the United States is 1-510-666-7889. His international headquarters is in London, England: +44 207 261 9049. His e-mail address is hq@lamassociation.org.

Classes and Workshops

Master Lam offers public classes in Piedmont, California. For information about current classes, please visit his website, http://www.lamkamchuen.com. Master Lam is willing to arrange, on request, workshops on qigong for specific conditions and illnesses. If you are interested in arranging a workshop for Master Lam anywhere in the world, please send a written proposal to hq@lamassociation.org.

Professional Seminars

If you are a health professional interested in the application of qigong in the care of people suffering from anxiety or other conditions, Master Lam is more than willing to discuss offering specialized professional seminars. If you are interested in arranging a professional seminar anywhere in the world with Master Lam, please send a written proposal to hq@lamassociation.org.

Websites

Master Lam's websites include:

http://www.lamhealing.com

This is the main website, where you will find details of the healing treatments that Master Lam offers using qigong and the other health systems in which he has been trained and that he has practiced throughout his life.

http://www.lamkamchuen.org

This is the principal website for the classes and workshops that Master Lam and his sons offer in the United States. It also provides helpful background on the healing tradition they preserve.

http://www.lamkamchuen.com

This is Master Lam's international website, which has extensive details on his art, his books and films, his classes, and his healing work worldwide.

http://www.lamassociation.org

This is the website of the Lam Association of Cultural Art, Europe. This is Master Lam's European hub. It includes detailed information about Master Lam and his activities in European countries as well as links to his qualified instructors.

Inner Strength
Anxiety Workshops and Personal Consultations with Master Lam

Physicians write over ninety-four million prescriptions for anti-anxiety medication annually in the United States alone.*

Whether you are taking medication, or receiving therapy for anxiety—or looking for a totally different treatment plan—the centuries-old qigong system of internal energy strengthening can help you. It offers a different, time-tested method for counteracting the destabilizing effects of anxiety. It builds your internal reservoir of inner strength while allowing you to continue with any other form of treatment you wish.

International qigong authority Master Lam offers workshops and personal consultations on request.

If you would like to arrange a workshop or personal consultation with Master Lam, please contact him. His phone number in the United States is 1-510-666-7889. His international headquarters is in London, England: +44 207 261 9049. His e-mail address is hq@lamassociation.org.

* Miller, Lisa. 2012. "Listening to Xanax." New York, March 18. http://nymag.com/news /features/xanax-2012-3/.

Books and Videos
with Master Lam

Through his books and videos Master Lam has introduced and taught a range of Chinese cultural arts in the West. His works have sold over a million copies, in seventeen languages. For copies of his books, please consult your local or online bookseller. For videos and DVDs, please contact Master Lam directly at http://www .lamkamchuen.org or e-mail hq@lamassociation.org.

The Way of Energy

A comprehensive qigong manual, the first book in Master Lam's trilogy. This is the groundbreaking work that introduced the zhan zhuang system of qigong to the Western world. This book provides an understanding of the human energy system, including practical exercises to help harness internal energy and stimulate blood circulation.

The Way of Healing

The second book in this trilogy presents a simple program of qigong and tai chi exercises to gently improve the inner energy flow, which is vital to good health. The routines are suitable for all ages and levels of fitness, and there are special modifications for people with disabilities and those who are in poor health.

The Way of Power

The third part of the trilogy introduces *Da Cheng Chuan* ("the great accomplishment"). This is the most powerful of all the martial arts. The book features classical qigong exercises, but also movements drawn from this extraordinary martial art.

Everyday Chi Kung

A program of seated qigong to fit in your day, at work, home, or play. Offering a fifteen-minute-a-day routine, this is the first book to focus on seated qigong.

Walking Chi Kung

A manual that focuses on qigong in motion and includes over fifteen different walking steps and systems.

Step-by-Step Tai Chi

The leading beginner's guide to this ancient art, featuring clear step-by-step instructions and color photographs of the basic tai chi movements.

Tai Chi for Staying Young

A simple exercise program for all ages, featuring careful, step-by-step descriptions of movements and exercises that can be performed as a daily routine at home or in any other convenient location.

The Feng Shui Handbook

This guide presents the philosophy of this art and shows how to use feng shui to bring harmonious energy into the home or office, thus promoting both health and general well-being.

The Personal Feng Shui Manual

A practical guide to creating your individual feng shui chart and direction finder to create harmony in everyday situations.

The Feng Shui Kitchen

The energy of food; feng shui essentials; preparing and cooking; and recipes for the four seasons.

The Way of Tea

A detailed guide to the art of making and enjoying this delicious, healthy, and complex drink.

Master Lam on Film

Stand Still—Be Fit

A ten-part television series that presents step-by-step qigong that stimulates the internal body, enhancing physical energy and promoting health and well-being. The complete series is available online at http://www.lamkamchuen.org/Simple_Exercise/Simple _Exercise.html.

The Way of Power

Filmed in China and London, it contains nearly fifty minutes of unique demonstrations by Master Lam, Professor Yu, Madame Wang Yuk Fong (daughter of Grand Master Wang Xiang Zhai), and students. It also includes a unique demonstration of internal power.

Golden Ball Tai Chi

Classical movement compiled by Master Lam for his students. Strengthens your body, clears your mind, and lifts your spirit. Filmed on locations with Master Lam teaching local citizens, it includes simple, rejuvenating exercises that can be done by people who need to sit or lie down.

References

"Anxiety." 2013. *Opinionator* (blog). *New York Times*. http://opinionator.blogs.nytimes.com/category/anxiety/.

"The Hubble Ultra Deep Field in 3D." YouTube video, 4:17, posted by "Deep Astronomy." August 2, 2009. http://www.youtube.com/watch?v=oAVjF_7ensg.

Miller, Lisa. 2012. "Listening to Xanax." *New York*, March 18. http://nymag.com/news/features/xanax-2012-3/.

Needham, Joseph, Ling Wang, and Kenneth Robinson. 1962. *Science and Civilisation in China*. Vol. 4, *Physics and Physical Technology*. Cambridge: Cambridge University Press.

Ricard, Matthieu, and Xuan Thuan Trinh. 2001. *The Quantum and the Lotus: A Journey to the Frontiers Where Science and Buddhism Meet*. New York: Crown.

Master Kam Chuen Lam has been a traditional Chinese healer for over forty years. He is also an internationally respected authority in the Chinese health systems of qigong and tai chi. He has produced over ten titles in these subjects and they have been sold across the world in over seventeen languages.

Grandmaster Yu Yongnian wrote the foreword to this workbook months before his death at age 94. He was the world's leading authority on the rare qigong system known as "standing like a tree." As a medical doctor trained in Western medicine, he brought the health benefits of this ancient system into hospitals and clinics throughout China. He was a member of China's National Qigong Research Council and was a consultant to the American-Chinese Qigong Research Group. He was also a consultant to the Da Cheng Chuan Zhan Zhuang Chi Kung Research Groups (Europe).

Professor Yu travelled and taught in both Asian and European countries. He supervised the production of Master Kam Chuen Lam's first book, *The Way of Energy*, and appears in both *The Way of Power* and its companion video in a rare demonstration of his teaching methods and power.